Vincent F. Hendricks • Pelle G. Hansen

Infostorms

How to Take Information Punches and Save Democracy

C

Copernicus Books

Vincent F. Hendricks
University of Copenhagen
Copenhagen
Denmark

Pelle G. Hansen
ISSP—Initiative for Science, Society & Policy
Roskilde University
Roskilde
Denmark

ISBN 978-3-319-03831-5   ISBN 978-3-319-03832-2 (eBook)
DOI 10.1007/978-3-319-03832-2
Springer Cham Heidelberg New York Dordrecht London

Library of Congress Control Number: 2013956504

Printed on acid-free paper

Springer is part of Springer Science+Business Media (www.springer.com)

For Horacio Arló-Costa:
an excellent mind
and a great friend, who passed on way too early

Preface

Writing this book has been all at once revitalizing, disheartening and harmonizing. Revitalizing because we as humans from time to time, in spite of the infostorms ravaging are nevertheless able to act rationally and differentiate between what is mere information and what is knowledge—the two are not mutually exclusive, nor are they necessarily convergent. Disheartening because ourselves, and what we think others think, social media, crowd-opinion systems, politicians, the press and many other bullhorns to the world often enough seduce us with incorrect information leading to disastrous decisions. Harmonizing, since the philosophical, logical, psychological and game theoretical considerations, on which this the book's analyses are based, appear to apply to real life phenomena and events that affect our everyday life and which we ought to be vigilant of.

Some material in this book has been lifted from "Infostorms", Hansen, P.G., Hendricks, V.F and Rendsvig, R.K., *Metaphilosophy*, vol. 44(3), April, 2013: 301–326 published by Wiley-Blackwell; the paper "Knowledge Transmissibility and Pluralistic Ignorance: A First Stab", Hendricks, V.F., *Metaphilosophy*, vol. 41(3), April, 2010: 279–291 also published by Wiley-Blackwell; the paper "Science Bubbles", Budtz Pedersen, D. and Hendricks, V.F., *Philosophy and Technology*, vol. 27(3): 359–372, published by Springer; the Danish book *Oplysningens blinde vinkler: En åndselitær kritik af informationssamfundet*, Hansen, P.G. and Hendricks, V.F., 2010 published by Samfundslitteratur, Copenhagen; and various columns appearing in Danish by Hendricks published in *Ingeniøren*, Copenhagen. We would like to thank the publishers for allowing us to reuse some of the material in *Infostorms*. Vincent F. Hendricks would like to thank the Velux Foundation for the grant *Humanomics: Mapping the Humanities* (grant nr. 437810) making much of the research to be found in this book possible.

For constructive comments, significant proposed amendments as well as encouragement, we would like to thank Alexandru Baltag, Robert A. Becker, Thomas Bestle, Thomas Bolander, Adam Brandenburger, Johan van Benthem, Henrik Boensvang, David Budtz Pedersen, Jerome L. Coben, Henriette Divert-Hendricks, Robin Engelhardt, Luciano Floridi, Nina Gierasimczuk, Joseph-Maria Hansen, Jeffrey Helzner, Maja Horst, Kevin T. Kelly, Hannes Leitgeb, Christian List, Fenrong

Liu, Jan Lundorff-Rasmussen, Teit Molter, Larry S. Moss, Søren Gosvig Olesen, Johan G. Olsen, Erik J. Olsson, Stig Andur Pedersen, Philip Pettit, Rie Smitha Bisgaard Pedersen, Frederik Preisler, Rasmus K. Rendsvig, Sonja Smets, Frederik Stjernefelt, John Symons, Dan Zahavi, Kevin Zollman and Gregory Wheeler.

Last but not least we would like to thank Milton W. Hendricks for some of the illustrations, our publisher Copernicus Books in New York City and Ties Nijssen from Springer for taking this project on.

September 2013   Vincent F. Hendricks
Copenhagen   Pelle G. Hansen

Testimonials

Infostorms uses examples and logic to offer a distinctive perspective on how everyday activities combined with public information may manipulate our actions, our opinions, or our choices of what to buy or sell. Their examples illustrate notions ranging from social proof, information cascades, opinion bubbles, pluralistic ignorance, framing and polarization effects, and bystander effects. The pages are full of summaries of experimental studies, anecdotes and simple models that challenge how we think of information, knowledge, and actions. This book should be read by everyone interested in network formation and researchers interested in decision making behavior.

Robert A. Becker, Professor of Economics, Indiana University, Bloomington

Informed fair decision making is not a fixed virtue that a democratic society acquires once and for all, it is a process that constantly needs rethinking and reshaping under changing circumstances. This highly original book brings the latest insights from logic, philosophy, social choice theory, cognitive psychology, and game theory to bear on the vast information streams that drive our lives. Its innovative unified perspective sensitizes the reader to the many informational whirlpools that can make us, and our societies, spin out of control, and it makes us better equipped to cope with them. The result is a showpiece of socially responsible fundamental science.

Johan van Benthem, Professor of Logic and Philosophy, University of Amsterdam & Stanford University

Infostorms is a sophisticated and accessible investigation into the crucial information flows that shape and govern so many aspects of our social, economic and political lives. It elegantly manages to select crucial results in a variety of technical fields, from logic to game theory, from economics to psychology, and make them cast new and much needed light on the infosphere. An interdisciplinary tour de force not to be missed.

Luciano Floridi, OII's Professor of Philosophy and Ethics of Information, University of Oxford and Fellow of St Cross College, Oxford

Modern man doesn't need more news—he needs better news. And journalists should learn that information is no longer a scarce resource. We all drown in the polluted information surrounding us. What people need is means of navigation, meaning and alignment. Infostorms is a thoughtful, well-written and scary warning to every media organization: Change!

Ulrik Haagerup, Executive Director of News, Danish Broadcasting Company

This is an unusual book with a wonderful collection of social phenomena that involve logical reasoning with important notions such as knowledge, information, and beliefs. I was particularly impressed by the nice balance between intriguing stories, formal analysis, and the insights conveyed by the authors. I am sure that readers will be enlightened by this book.

Fenrong Liu, Professor of Logic, Tsinghua University, Beijing

We live in environments that are rich in information, soundbites, and noise. Our highly connected social networks facilitate the transmission of information, but can also contribute to the spread of misinformation and even disinformation. To build strong democracies and flourishing liberal societies, we must understand how our information environments function and what challenges and opportunities they generate. Written by two scholars with a strongly interdisciplinary orientation, this book brings together insights from many different academic fields to shed light on the mechanisms underpinning information flows in society and how we might respond to them. It is a highly recommended read for social scientists and concerned citizens alike.

Christian List, Professor of Political Science and Philosophy, London School of Economics

A highly readable book, *Infostorms* is aimed as much at "students" in the broad sense as those at the university. It is sure to provoke wide-ranging discussions in classrooms. In addition, its themes and examples suggest new research questions. All in all, it is an important contribution to the social sciences for both the academy and the public.

Lawrence S. Moss, Professor of Mathematics, Indiana University Program in Pure and Applied Logic

We now make our democratic decisions, as we live our everyday lives, buffeted by gales of purported information that are stronger and more wayward than any previous generation has had to weather. Drawing on many different disciplines and traditions, *Infostorms* offers an analysis of these forces that is indispensable for everyone who is invested, as we all should be, in the value and the future of democracy.

Philip Pettit, L.S. Rockefeller University Professor of Politics and Human Values, Princeton University; University Distinguished Professor of Philosophy, Australian National University

Contents

About the Authors

Vincent F. Hendricks is Professor of Formal Philosophy at The University of Copenhagen. He is editor-in-chief of Synthese: *An International Journal for Epistemology, Methodology and Philosophy of Science* and was awarded the *Elite Research Prize* by the Danish Ministry of Science, Technology and Innovation in 2008.

Pelle G. Hansen is Behavioral Researcher at Roskilde University; Director of ISSP—*The Initiative of Science, Society & Policy* at Roskilde University and University of Southern Denmark; and member of the Prevention Council of the Danish Diabetes Assoc. He also heads the collaborative venture www.iNudgeYou.com and is chairman of the Danish Nudging Network.

Chapter 1
Introduction and Manipulation

The information in the world doubles everyday. What they don't tell us, is that our wisdom is cut in half at the same time.

—Joey Novick

"I don't get swung by what other people have to say about this and that; I get information from a variety of sources, weigh the pros against the cons, triangulate intelligence, ask some more questions to peers and public, counterbalance positive and negative reviews online, analyze the evidence and then equitably and without emotion deliberate, decide and act for myself. I do so all the time; it doesn't matter whether we're talking about the routine of selecting my new cell phone or which party to vote for in the next election. That's all I have to say about that!"

Unfortunately, that's not all there is to say about that even though the information age provides virtual oceans of information. First of all, information on which trivial as well crucial decisions are based may be tampered with, and second personal belief, deliberation, decision and action are influenced by what other people think or do. The aggregated opinion of others may influence our personal viewpoint. In *Science*, a paper was recently published (Muchnik et al. 2013) describing a randomized experiment on a social news aggregator platform and online rating system, the result of which testifies to massive social influence bias on individual users. On an unidentified crowd-based opinion aggregator system ostensibly "similar to Digg.com and Reddit.com", the status of 101,281 comments made by users over a 5 month period with more than 10 million views and rated 308,515 times, was monitored. In collaboration with the service, the researchers had rigged the setup in such a way that whenever a user left a comment it was automatically rendered with either a positive upvote, a negative downvote or no vote at all for control. Now, here is a key of the experiment: If a comment received *just a single* upvote, the likelihood of receiving another upvote for the first user to see it was 32% relative to the control group. Additionally chances were also higher that such comments would proliferate in, or lemming to, popularity as the upvote group on average had a 25% greater rating than the control group. One of the lessons from this experiment is that

> attempts to aggregate collective judgment and socialize choice could be easily manipulated, with dramatic consequences for our markets, our politics, and our health (Muchnik et al. 2013, p. 351).

V. F. Hendricks, P. G. Hansen, *Infostorms,* DOI 10.1007/978-3-319-03832-2_1, © Springer International Publishing Switzerland 2014

It is hardly news that others influence us; it is hardly news that we are susceptible to social information phenomena like herding, lemming-effects, cascades, bystander-effects, group-thinking, collective boom-thinking etc. But it is news that modern information technologies have magnified and amplified phenomena for which social information processes threaten to distort truth, making us more vulnerable to err than ever and on a much larger scale. The abundance of information driven by technologies such as computers and in particular the World Wide Web has forced us to increasingly rely on information technologies that short-cut traditional cumbersome search processes that cannot cope with the plenitude of available information as well as offering tempting avenues for by-passing traditional slow gate-keepers of correct information. Relying more and more on social media, crowd-based opinion generators and other online "democratic" rating, comment or information acquisition systems not only makes such side-tracking possible and more likely to occur; it also increases the numerical, if not the proportional, reach of the spreading of false beliefs and consequences thereof—intentionally or non-intentionally. When this happens, the resulting phenomena are referred to as an *infostorm*.

While the social information phenomena magnified by such technologies have always existed, they now take on new proportions with possible severe consequences for the democratic institutions underpinning the information societies we live in. The more we uncritically rely on automatic information technologies, the more likely it is that the consequences go unnoticed, sometimes with absurd results.

While the described experiment perhaps doesn't have severe consequences for our democratic institutions, it exemplifies what may happen to the reflection of truth when we solicit our decision making power to, and rely unconditionally on, information technologies and processes. In other cases the result of relying on such processes may amplify information phenomena that track truth imperfectly in ways that give us reasons to believe the truly unbelievable with severe consequences for science and society.

1.1 Democracy, Information and Knowledge

It is often claimed that the information age, with its crowd- based information aggregators, has "democratized" knowledge. But knowledge and information are not the same.

Plato had a hard time with democracy because truth can't be determined by majority vote. The amount of articles, the number of information sites and individuals who read and contribute to them do not as such guarantee the truth of the information passed along by social media and crowd news, opinion and rating dynamos. Plato was also aware of the essential difference between information and knowledge. By way of example, you may be informed, or convinced, of the world being ruled by narrow-minded vested financial interests without knowing it. But if you know the world is ruled by narrow-minded money vested interests, you are also informed of this. *Knowledge implies information, but information doesn't necessarily imply knowledge.* Knowledge is required to track the truth, but no such relation is required for belief, conviction or information. Tracking the truth is not fixed by whatever the majority think, hope, and feel or what the population at large is informed of. Besides truth, the way in which information is *processed* presents a crucial difference between knowledge and information. In short *knowledge=reliable process+true information* and the capabilities and information dynamics of the crowd are not always a reliable knowledge acquisition process.

The good thing about knowledge is that even though it might be a real hassle to obtain, it does stick around and may henceforth be used for deliberation, decision and action with respect to a variety of different problems. Meanwhile one must first get to know the tools in the toolbox, and that may yet again be a challenge of hardship. That's just too bad: *knowledge is contrary to, for instance, wiki-information or socially aggregated opinion, not democratic, but a regime.*

It is a different story with information. It may be procured easily, quickly and cheaply. The problem is that we can't just solve climate problems, the challenge in the Middle East or democratic disagreement, no matter how many we are or how quickly we may compile and read articles, entries, comments and their up- or downvotes on the web. Many may coincidentally share the same view at the same time, and jack it up further by additional ratings, but this doesn't guarantee a solution to the problems at hand nor ensure that there is anything correct about the positive consensus. For such problems we must venture down the knotty road of knowledge.

The shibboleth of the age of Enlightenment was *sapere aude* (dare to know). The expression implied that if not downright dangerous, then it was at least challenging and labour-intensive to obtain knowledge. Knowledge is not something one herds. It is something one *acquires*, knowledge requires protocol and procedure and that's precisely why one cannot equate knowledge with information.

The American physicist and priest, William Pollard, is quoted as having said:

> Information is a source of learning. But unless it is organized, processed, and available to the right people in a format for decision-making, it is a burden, not a benefit.

Similarly, the founder of the Lotus Development Corporation, Mitchell Kapor, is reported to have proclaimed:

> Getting information off the Internet is like taking a drink from a fire hydrant.

It's so easy to hoard information these days, but it by no means follows that decisive decisions have become easier to make, or that apprehension and insight may be taken for granted by the mere quantity of information. Organizing, processing and formatting information correctly as required for knowledge-based decision proficiency requires tools, assessment, evaluation and the audacity the thinkers of the Enlightenment spoke of.

This may seem paradoxical. Had Spinoza, Kant and the rest of the philosophers of the Enlightenment predicted that all this effort would end in an age of information where free and savvy citizens are exceedingly susceptible to social influence, crowd-aggregated points of view and opinion bubbles, they would have been dreaming of the spirit and times of the dark Middle Ages, which they had worked so hard to rid society of.

Former US Ambassador to the United Nations and sociologist, Daniel P. Moynihan, once purportedly said:

You're entitled to your own opinions, but you are not entitled to your own facts.

Knowledge *must* respect the facts and thereby the truth. Information doesn't necessarily have to, and opinions, well, they are sometimes free of charge. They may easily be produced at little or no cost, without respecting anything much but still be rather robust and decisive for individual and group reasoning.

1.2   Manipulation

This is not to say that crowd-reasoning, socially aggregated opinion and joint-rating aggregators always lead us astray. The masses may every so often get it exactly right and indeed many minds may produce knowledge (Sunstein 2006). It is to say however that an array of *socio-informational phenomena* reputable to philosophy, logic, economics, game theory and social psychology (Hendricks and Rendsvig 2014b) indeed may cloud collective judgement, reason and rationality. The heavy reliance on information technological services doesn't help one bit but only makes the whole environment in which we reason and act much more hospitable to infostorms. Even worse, furnished with adequate knowledge of these phenomena and the ways in which they may be deployed, one may derail or in other ways exploit human cognition and profoundly influence people's decisions in numerous different matters, varying from shopping for a new freezer chest, to who one should vote for during the next parliamentary election. Information may consequently be used to manipulate people, opinions and markets.

Based on an example package from political, economic, cultural and social reality, the following chapters examine an important bouquet of these information phenomena. The purpose of the exercise is to provide

1. an analysis of the information phenomena's structure, and how
2. knowledge of the structure and dynamics may be used to control people, their opinions and the disparate markets in which they operate, in an attempt to establish
3. a number of "junior woodchuck codes" or rules of thumb pertaining to what one should be aware of as an edified citizen, and
4. why it becomes more important than ever before to be able to draw the line between knowledge and information as each relates to deliberation, decision and action both individually and collectively.

1.3   Social Proof

Humans acquire information from at least two sources: From our immediate environment and what our senses dictate and from what other agents apparently decide to believe or do. In case of uncertainty as to what to believe or do, individual agents try to tap the immediate environment for more information to become wiser or facilitate qualified decision. But when the environment has no more information to offer or for some reason or the other bars additional tapping, agents may decide to consult or observe other agents. This latter source of information is known as *social proof* in social psychology (Cialdini 2007) and may be an extremely influential vehicle for deliberation, decision and action individually and jointly: *Single agents assume beliefs, norms or actions of other agents in an attempt to reflect the correct view, stance, behavior for a given situation.*

Social proof may be conceived as an information source or resource. Sometimes social proof gives a lot, sometimes little guidance as to what to think or do depending on both the quality and quantity of information available from others. The quality and quantity distinction is in part responsible for distinguishing between different information phenomena, which may influence decision-making. Crudely, *too little* information or *too much*, the way in which information is *presented* to a deciding body, and finally the way in which information is *sorted* may all in different ways come into play and generate unfortunate collective situations.

1.4 Info-Outline

Chapter 2 deals with *pluralistic ignorance, bystander-effects* and *informational cascades.* These phenomena emerge when people observe other people's actions or opinions in the attempt to figure out what they themselves should do. The danger of pluralistic ignorance arises when each decision-maker in a group has too little information to solve a given problem, and instead of scrutinizing the issue, further observes others in the hope of becoming wiser. But when everyone else does the same, everyone simply observes the lack of reaction, and therefore based on this very lack of reaction easily makes a wrong inference. The general reaction fails to materialize which makes precisely the lack of reaction appear as legit or acceptable— the centerpiece of the bystander-effect. Once you have discovered how to establish such situations or states of collective mind, and moreover have an interest in establishing them, you can grossly exploit them to swing over public opinion, create false agreement, cyber-bully on the web, carry out sudden and comprehensive changes or make hordes of consumers buy designated products.

Just as pluralistic ignorance is established when each person observes the remainder of the group's reaction, manipulation may also occur by means of a chain reaction of too much information from the surroundings. Such an *informational cascade* transpires when people one by one adopt the opinions or actions of passers-by as valid examples of what to think or do. It can yet again be quite rational to compensate for one's lack of knowledge in such a way, but just like pluralistic ignorance, the outcome may turn out to be rather petrifying. Taking others' choices as definitive testimony may end up trumping over individual substantiated doubt, true information, rational decision or correct judgment of the situation. One can thus end up reproducing others' mistakes, or jump on a wagon without anyone knowing where it's heading.

Of course lemming along unreflectively may be additionally accentuated by modern information technologies until the barometer reads infostorm.

Pluralistic ignorance, bystander-effects and information cascades make it clear that the one who controls the *public space* and its embedded information can do a lot of good, but also do a lot of damage. This begs the question of what the public space is, how it's related to information and knowledge, as well as what value the public space has in everyday life and in matters of democracy. It turns out that the public space is closely interconnected with a special sort of knowledge, called *common knowledge*, and the purpose of Chap. 3 is to uncover the connection between public space and common knowledge.

The public space is a cornerstone of democracy, a space which may be tampered with through information control. However, it is not the only democratic cornerstone one can move around using various information phenomena and ploys as vehicles. What our own role in society should be, and what it requires to act the part, is another. In recent years, the perception of free will has been a major draw card, where both the left and right leg of the political spectrum have been tripping over one another in pure zeal. But what is actually called for, before a choice may be referred to as free? This is explored in Chap. 4, since what the free choice amounts to evidently plays a pivotal role when living in a democracy where one may 'freely' decide who one votes for.

There may be more than enough information available to the citizen, the voter or the decision-maker, but if the information is *presented* in a certain way, it may also be used for unpleasant manipulative purposes. In Chap. 5, the so-called *framing effect* is the focal point. If people are asked to choose between two (or more) alternatives, which they are fully informed of, and where the two alternatives cause the same net result, their decision may ultimately be influenced by how the alternative choices are presented or framed. If you can influence an individual's choice or decision solely by the way the choices are set out, you can make people do pretty much anything. You may get people to reverse their preferences or make choices which either don't benefit them or are downright inconsistent—meaning that you in the same situation choose options which are not able to be fulfilled simultaneously.

Where the framing effect is based on information presentation, another uncomfortable phenomenon of collective bias is the result of *information selection*. Chapter 6 disentangles the phenomenon of *polarization,* where people's attitudinal agreement is strengthened when further processing the available information in terms of deliberation or debate. Therefore if a group is in agreement on a certain topic, whether political, religious, cultural or otherwise, they have a tendency to only view and consider information which endorses their already established opinions. There is a weighty sorting of what information and which voices one is willing to listen to. In this way an echo chamber may appear where one exclusively listens to others who have the same viewpoint as oneself. The more echoes heard, and the more information supporting one's own position, the more likely it is to become convinced that you yourself are right, and everyone else is simply wrong. The worst-case scenario is that this form of polarization leads to extremism, hate, violence, even terror or war. This may be alarming enough, however in addition polarization can threaten a societal ideal valued very highly, that is, the ideal of the *deliberative democracy*, where multi-faceted expression of opinions and mature exchange of views precedes decisions in democratic matters. Similarly to the previous chapters on pluralistic ignorance, informational cascades and framing effects, this chapter clarifies how polarization may threaten deliberative democracy and robust social order.

Informational cascades and irrational herding have proven to be part of the explanation for real-estate or stock bubbles in financial markets. Unfortunate aggregated opinion about the value of an asset has overheated the asset far beyond its fundamental value. At some point, the bubble may burst. The bubble phenomenon is not only characteristic in finance; indeed, one may speak of opinion bubbles, political bubbles, social bubbles, status bubbles, fashion bubbles, art bubbles even science bubbles. Chapter 7 takes you through the bubble universe with particular emphasis on science and opinion bubbles on the "free" market of convictions.

If pluralistic ignorance, bystander-effects, informational cascades, framing effects and polarization are allowed to ravage along with other information phenomena, one runs the risk of becoming intellectually blind, deaf and mute and altogether may face insurmountable problems while trying to navigate rationally as citizen, voter, consumer. In fact passing as human rather than lemming may be hard if social proof becomes unreflectively too pronounced. Chapter 8 provides a concrete analysis of how the lack of understanding of the frames that we as voters reason and act within may end up leading us astray and into dead ends. Chapter 9 uncovers the informational structure of—and mechanics behind—an array of diverse societal phenomena, ranging from blood donation and ghettoization to consumer democracy.

The picture sketched is rather depressing. It seems that we as humans, citizens and decision-makers are just handed over to a long line of information phenomena and different ploys that others at their discretion may use to delude and derail us— and then but amplify using current information technology. But we are not always victims of the hands of malice in our daily doings, and from time to time it's possible to negotiate the maze of information just fine. So despite the luring infostorms we are often still able to differentiate between relevant, sufficient and well-balanced correct information, including knowledge about our limits of knowledge on one hand, and incomplete, selective or distorted information on the other. Information may both strengthen and undermine democratic processes depending on how the information is being used. But knowledge and democracy do not have a similarly strained relationship between them. Knowledge as a combination of truthful information and reliable processes on one hand and democracy on the other turn out to be interdependent issues, a point substantiated in Chap. 10.

Chapter 2
Ignorance and Cascades

The more you can create that magic bubble, that suspension of disbelief, for a while, the better.

—Edward Norton

2.1 Computer City

Computer City sells plenty of interesting gizmos and gadgets. So one day, Vincent went there and for reasons unknown fell in love with a small laptop, even though he is already the proud owner of four or five of them. As a good and informed consumer he asked the shop assistant various questions to acquire more information about the product.

What concerned Vincent that day was the following: A computer may have quite a high clock frequency and therefore be rather fast internally in the processor, but if the 'highway' (called the *bus*) on which data is transmitted from the processor to other central parts of the computer has a much lower clock frequency or speed limit, then it means zilch. It's equivalent to driving a Ferrari Testarossa in first gear with the lever-brake pulled. You get a bottleneck. Therefore Vincent naturally asked the shop assistant:

- Excuse me, what's the clock frequency on the bus for this laptop?
- I have no clue whatsoever!
- But since you are selling the product wouldn't it perhaps be nice to know, or what?
- Listen! I don't think you may find a single one of my colleagues in the store who knows it either.

At this reply Vincent turned crimson-faced with rage, and hurled candid oaths and curses at the shop assistant's reasoning, which apparently came down to:

1. None of my colleagues know, and therefore you have no reason to *expect* that I know; and
2. None of my colleagues know, and therefore you have no reason to expect that I *should* know.

Granted, a tacit premise is in play to the effect that shop assistants know, or at least should know, what is valuable for the consumer to know about a certain product. But by the above reasoning, in contrast, it now seems to apply that Vincent naturally shouldn't be critical of the shop assistant's ignorance of what the clock frequency on the bus was, since one may no longer expect that shop assistants know such things,

V. F. Hendricks, P. G. Hansen, *Infostorms*, DOI 10.1007/978-3-319-03832-2_2,
© Springer International Publishing Switzerland 2014

or think they ought to know them. In this light it seems completely legitimate for all parties to remain ignorant about the clock frequency on the bus! What a travesty.

Alas, just because something *appears* reasonable, it doesn't *need* to be, and that's exactly why Vincent's face assumed a, for him, hitherto unaccustomed color.

The reasoning in item (1) is an example of a rudimentary fallacious inductive inference. One cannot logically infer from the fact that some ravens are black, that all ravens are black. Just because *some* shop assistants don't have knowledge of the product specifications doesn't imply that *all* shop assistants in Computer City—and especially not the shop assistant who is specifically in charge of selling laptops—are equally ignorant. Thus, Vincent did have good reason to expect that the shop assistant would be able to answer the question.

But item (2) is even more interesting: Firstly because it occasioned the shop assistant's indignation, and secondly because it constitutes the body of the information phenomenon known as *pluralistic ignorance*.

2.2 Today's Lesson: Pluralistic Ignorance

The concept *pluralistic ignorance* was originally developed by psychologists Daniel Katz and Floyd H. Allport and refers to

> a situation where the majority of group members privately rejects the norm, but assumes (incorrectly) that most others accept it (Katz and Allport 1931, p. 152).

This distinct configuration of personal beliefs about other people's beliefs may quickly turn inopportune. Most people as a rule assume—and often for good reason—that there indeed may be some merit in considering information pertaining to what other people believe or think you should do, before you decide what you personally should believe or do. But when pluralistic ignorance enters, this way of thinking may however lead to each individual in the end assenting to a certain norm, without he or she personally believing it justified.

Generally, pluralistic ignorance may arise when a group of decision-makers attempts to form an opinion at one and the same time based on a *public signal*. When you ask a newly commenced class of philosophy students gathered in a lecture hall if there was anyone who didn't grasp today's homework assignment, it's often the case that no one raises their hand, despite the fact that today's homework assignment is an extract from Martin Heidegger's labyrinthine *Sein und Zeit*.

The lack of hands naturally seems strange, since each student presumably has an honest interest in exchanging confusion for clarity. Yet in deciding whether you should signify your ignorance or doubt, each student initially discreetly looks around to see whether there are others who have apparently had similar problems in grasping the homework assignment of the day. When all students do so simultaneously, everyone receives the same public signal, that is, no one apparently shares their problem. So the act of orientation itself creates a powerful public signal, which distorts the truth. To avoid damaging their reputation, each student accordingly chooses *not* to

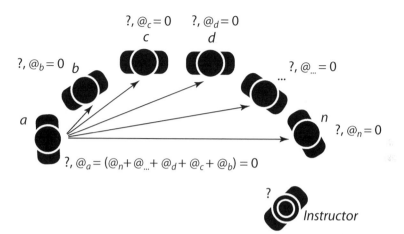

? Public signal
@ Choice = 0 or 1

Fig. 2.1 A simple mechanism for establishing a state of pluralistic ignorance with n persons, who all receive a public signal "?" from the instructor and must make a choice or decision "@", where 1 denotes raising a hand, while 0 means to refrain from doing so. Each of the n persons observes others and each reacts like person a, who doesn't raise a hand since there is no one else doing so and so it goes

raise their hand. In other words: Everyone omits acting on his or her personal knowledge concerning lack of the selfsame, because no one directly acts based on their personal ignorance, doubt or confusion due to the information in the public signal, that the very act of orientation transmits (Fig. 2.1).

The experienced student has of course learned to see through this mist. But that is not necessarily a great help to him or her, since one lonesome hand still exhibits the person in question as a lonely ignorant. Thus even experienced students often display this sort of behavior to avoid unfortunate exhibition and conform to the herd.

The experienced instructor, on the other hand, generally knows both how to exploit or handle this phenomenon. If you wish to avoid questions from the hall, you may just phrase or frame your question as just witnessed. If you instead wish to share your knowledge, you may for instance ask the students what they think most *former* students have had for problems with the specified homework assignment. By framing the question accordingly, you may avoid the first hand in the air becoming a display of ignorance. What the instructor is really doing to drive an answer from the students in this case is to remove the orientation act (forcing social proof when in individual doubt) creating the wrongful public signal.

Back to Computer City and the possibly dense reasoning of the shop assistant:

> None of my colleagues have information about the clock frequency on the bus; therefore I don't have reason to be informed about it. And therefore you as a consumer don't have reason to expect to be informed on this subject either.

It now becomes evident that this is a case of pluralistic ignorance, where the Computer City assistant endorses a norm of ignorance, without he himself necessarily upon closer reflection finding it reasonable. For even though all Computer City assistants individually would find it relevant to know the clock frequency on the bus, and even though they probably also would find it entirely proper that the consumer asks about it, it follows from the norm that no one has sat down and tried to figure it out, since they are seemingly not expected to know it. Pluralistic ignorance is a collective state of erroneous belief.

Pluralistic ignorance thus explains the shop assistant's lack of information about the computer details. In the recurring daily way to orientate himself, none of his colleagues has expressed that there is any sort of reason why he should know the clock frequency on the bus. Therefore the shop assistant finds it both just and acceptable that he doesn't know it. The problem though is that good customers may quickly end up exposing a shop assistant's ignorance by calling attention to the relevance of that which he is ignorant of. Customers tend to ask, if they are in doubt. As a sales clerk you can always attempt to make the customer believe that he or she is stupid by stating a couple of fallacious arguments. It is after all never pleasant for someone to have his or her ignorance exposed about what turns out to be obviously relevant.

2.3   C'mon!

Pluralistic ignorance also features as an essential explanatory factor in the so-called *bystander-effect*. The bystander-effect expresses that the more individuals who are gathered in one place, the less is the likelihood of people coming to the aid of a person in need. When an emergency situation occurs, it is on the contrary more likely that a person comes to the rescue if there are fewer or almost no witnesses to the accident: "C'mon, you're standing right next to me!"

If one must fall, get badly hurt and be in need of assistance anywhere, then it's better that it happens on a quiet residential street in Park Slope, Brooklyn, where it's almost desolate, than if it happens on Times Square in Manhattan where thousands pass by on a daily basis.

Most people, upon hearing about the bystander-effect for the first time, generally have some trouble quite believing it. Meanwhile in a series of classic experiments, psychologists Bibb Latané and John Darley (1969) discovered that the time it takes for the trial subjects in a room to react and try to help is acutely sensitive to the number of people present. In one of the experiments the trial subjects were placed in the following scenarios:

1. Alone in a room,
2. With two other trial subjects, or
3. With two "co-conspirators", who passed themselves off as being regular trial subjects.

In each of these scenarios the trial subjects were set a questionnaire to answer. While the subjects now sat neck-deep in questions, the room started to fill up with smoke.

The question was now, how the trial subjects would react to this, depending on which one of the scenarios immediately above they found themselves in.

The results showed that when the trial subjects were alone 75 % of them reported the smoke, while only 38 % called attention to the smoke if there were two other trial subjects present. Most alarmingly though is that in the last scenario, where the two co-conspirators were present, *only 10 %* of the participants pointed out the smoke filling the room. These results in spite of the fact that the participants had noticed the smoke yet subsequently ignored it because everybody else apparently did.

An important factor in the bystander-effect is, therefore, that the presence of other people seemingly gives rise to confusion about responsibility. Since there are other people around, each individual is less pressed to take action, given that the responsibility for taking action is assumed to be evenly distributed amongst those present.

One may be tempted to think that when a single person realizes that the others aren't acting on their responsibility, then the entire burden of responsibility falls back on the particular person in question. Such a realization would cause the individual to act. But if a situation is *ambiguous*, the observation of others' lack of action may lead one to believe that there is no reason at all to take action or responsibility.

In a case of much heated debate from New York City in the 1960s, the 28-year-old Catherine "Kitty" Genovese was assaulted and stabbed on the stoop to her front door. It happened despite scores of neighbors who witnessed large parts of this horrific chain of events, which lasted over half an hour. Subsequently the press reported that no less than 38 witnesses had admitted that they had omitted to act or call the police. In the public debate that followed, the common reader had no doubt as to what the explanation was: Like any other metropolis, New York City had made its citizens callous and indifferent towards fellow citizens.

Looking closer at the press reconstruction of the neighbors' own explanations, it was however the fact that no one else seemed to have reacted, that had caused people to refrain from acting. The lack of reaction had instead made everyone believe that it wasn't a case of definite assault, but rather two lovers quarrelling (Manning et al. 2007). In other words, it was the ambiguity of the situation coupled with confusion over responsibility and pluralistic ignorance, which lead to this tragic example of the bystander-effect. That is, when others don't react, the individual views this information as a sign that a reaction is neither required nor socially demanded. The ironic point at the end of the day *is that no one does anything, precisely because no one does anything.*

2.4   The Structure of Bystander-Effects

The logical structure behind a bystander-effect includes (Hansen et al. 2013):

1. A set of agents that act concurrently in a number of rounds.
2. Three possible actions in each round.
3. A preference order on the outcome of choices.

A_s Action of agent s
! Public signal
$@_s$ Public signal for agent c from actions of previous agents

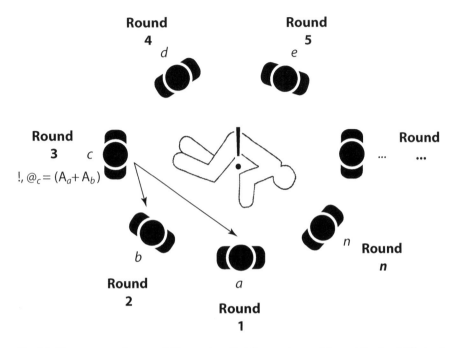

Fig. 2.2 The structure of a potential bystander-effect for agent c receiving public signal "!" about an emergency and a public signal "$@_c$" consisting of the actions "A_a" and "A_b" of agents a and b in previous rounds

Consider a set of witnesses to an emergency, who act simultaneously in a number of rounds. They can choose to either *help*, *not help* or *inquire further* to obtain more information. All agents prefer to help if help is required, but not help otherwise, i.e., their preference in choice depends on the true state of the world. If an agent chooses to help or not to help, the agent cannot choose in later rounds. It is however cost-free to "skip a round" by inquiring further or surveying the situation.

The decision is made under uncertainty: Agents do not know whether the situation in fact calls for assistance or not. There is no strategic interaction in the decision problem, so no agent will have an incentive to mislead subsequent agents by choosing in contrast to the best of their knowledge. Therefore the choices of other agents may be interpreted as conveying information regarding others' interpretation of the situation.

Now, agents may choose to base their action not only on their private information, but also on the information extracted from their peers—social proof. The following assumptions are made pertaining to the information dynamical structure (see also Fig. 2.2):

1. The underlying structure is known to all agents.
2. Each agent makes a rational decision in each round based on the available information, which consists of
   a. A *public signal* about the true state of the world,
   b. A *public signal* consisting of the actions *performed* by the previous agents.
3. A belief among the agents that others
   a. Given that they believe help is required, are more likely to help, than they are likely to either inquire or not help,
   b. Given that they believe help is not required, are more likely to not help, than they are likely to either survey or help, and
4. Knowledge of rationality as described in 2.

Pertaining to item (2), three things to note: First, in (2a), agents are assumed to receive a public signal about the true state of affairs. This signal consists of the emergency event, e.g., a visual impression that an elderly lady falls. This signal is assumed to be common knowledge, as everybody can see that everybody else can see the event, etc. But, it is not known to other agents how the individual agent *interprets* this signal. Second, agents are not assumed to be made aware by the end of a round whether their actions were in accordance with the true state of affairs. That is, no external source of information is available between rounds to inform agents in later rounds. Third, notice the emphasis in (2b): It is not only assumed that agents perceive the choice, and not the private signal, of other agents, but also that they only perceive the *performed output* of this choice. This is essential, as the choices to survey and to not help are *output equivalent.*

The assumption made in item (3) amounts to the fact that the group of agents are neck-deep in pluralistic ignorance with respect to the decision rules used in the situation. This is exactly the situation "where a majority of group members privately reject a norm, but assume (incorrectly) that most others accept it" (Centola et al. 2005, p. 1010), but where the norm in question is not a true social norm, but rather a decision rule. In conjunction with suitable assumptions regarding payoff and degrees of belief, *every agent will have a propensity to survey the situation instead of helping or not helping.* However, qua (3), all agents also believe that others reason by a *different* choice rule, namely that they would choose to help or not help under the same circumstances.

Let's have a test run of this simple setup. Consider three agents witnessing an event where an elderly woman trips in the street. Assume that the agents have 2 rounds to decide whether or not to help. The fact of the matter is that the lady needs help. The public signal sent by the event is, however, ambiguous: It may be interpreted as the lady tripping without being hurt or as the lady having badly twisted her ankle. Assume that all agents interpret the signal correctly, and therefore initially believe that the lady requires assistance.

Focus on a particular agent, *a*. Given that *a* believes that she is no better at interpreting the public signal than others it will be reasonable for her to survey. By surveying, *a* can observe the actions of others, and thereby gather information regarding their interpretation of the public signal. Under the assumption that others are at least as good as she is in estimating the true state from the public signal, this further information will lead to a stronger basis upon which she can later choose to either help or not help.

Notice how the reasoning for choosing to survey implicitly utilizes the assumption of pluralistic ignorance from (3) above. For *a* to be able to infer information from other agents' actions in the first round, it must be assumed that these actions reflect the agents' private beliefs, even though the action chosen by *a* does not convey her own beliefs to others.

To see how *a*'s action misrepresents her beliefs to others recall the assumption in (2b) above, stating that agents perceive the *performed output* of the choices of other agents. In the presented case, the choice to survey and the choice not to help are *output equivalent*: Other agents cannot distinguish these two choices from each other, as both outcomes consist in staying put and witnessing the situation at hand. Following the assumption of pluralistic ignorance, all other agents now believe that *a* has chosen *not to help*.

Given that all agents have acted as *a* did in the first round, what new information is *a* left with after she is done surveying the situation? She has seen two other witnesses not doing anything, and as she, due to pluralistic ignorance, believes that they follow a different choice rule than she, she will infer that they both interpreted the public signal to show that the true state is one in which no help is required. As this goes for all agents, a situation of *belief-oriented* pluralistic ignorance again has occurred: a situation in which "no one believes, but everyone thinks that everyone [else] believes [that no help is required]" (Krech and Crutchfield 1948, pp. 388–389).

As *a* takes the two other witnesses to be her peers, she will now have compelling reasons for revising her belief. Since the roles of all agents are symmetric, agent *a* is not a special case though, and hence the second round will commence with all three agents believing that no help is required. They can obtain nothing from surveying further (as this is the last round), so the rational choice will be to *not help*.

So a group of rational witnesses suffering from pluralistic ignorance regarding each others' decision rules may by social proof cause a bystander-effect.

2.5 "Todding"

Amanda Todd was a 15-year-old girl from Port Coquitlam, British Columbia, who took her own life on October 10, 2012. She was the victim of extensive and prolonged cyber-bullying on Facebook, YouTube and other social media platforms. Her last name has now occasioned the coining of a new, and quite morbid, expression on the web—"todding". Todding apparently now refers to loathsome and abhorrent campaigns against selected individuals on the web. After being exposed to such campaigns for some time, the victims (often teenagers) may develop everything from stress, depression, and anxiety attacks to substance abuse problems. For Amanda Todd, the result was suicide. She is probably not the first, and unlikely the last, who will kill herself as a result of "todding".

On September 7, 2012, Amanda Todd posts a video on YouTube entitled "My Story: Struggling, Bullying, Suicide and Self Harm". Using queue cards she tells her story of the cyber-bullying she has been exposed to for a long period of time. Almost instantly the video goes viral and is shown more than 1,600,000 times worldwide to the day of her death. The media picks it up, shows it, and online newspapers "like" the video too. But nobody intervenes for real despite all the views, comments, announcements of sympathy and concern and "likes".[1]

Amanda Todd's attempt to reach the public succeeded in the sense that a great many people apparently witnessed her cry for help, yet no one intervened for real. Why? There are two interconnected reasons for the lack of intervention. Views, comments and "likes" are cost neutral in the sense that the virtual disapproval of the horrific treatment of Amanda Todd and the terrible course of bullying events don't commit the individual to real intervention. Since the individual, private user as well as public media, observe that everybody else is disapproving without committing to intervention, then it becomes legitimate, indeed the norm, to disapprove and sympathize with Amanda Todd in this very way. This is the case even if every individual privately thinks that more should be done. Thus one comes to subscribe publicly to a norm one privately finds questionable just because "no one believes, but everyone thinks that everyone believes." That's pluralistic ignorance again and it doesn't get any better while everybody stands on the sideline watching how the ignorance uncontrollably goes viral and thus personally contributes to the *bystander-apathy* by a supporting "like".

On October 13, 2012, the day after Amanda Todd's suicide, "R.I.P. Amanda Todd" becomes a worldwide trend on Twitter. After her cry of distress on YouTube more than 700,000 Facebook-users had liked Amanda Todd's Facebook memorial page—now it is over a million. Despite this vast number of sympathizers there were still former classmates and trolls who added scornful comments like "I'm so happy she is dead". Amanda Todd had attempted to take her own life on an earlier occasion by drinking bleach before her father found her in a ditch. Home from the hospital after this sad incident she collected comments on social media like "She deserved it. Did you wash the mud out of your hair? I hope she is dead"[2] and an ad with the text "Clorox— it's to die for" with Amanda Todd's face superimposed on a person standing with a Clorox bottle in hand. Even after she committed suicide by hanging herself, bullies were still haunting her, posting photos on her memorial pages of bleach, ditches and hangmen with comments like "R.I.P Amanda Todd. I hope they sell Clorox in Hell."[3] On October 15, 2012 the Clorox Company issued a statement condemning

---

[1] More than 1,600,000 viewed Amanda Todd's video prior to her death, the count is up to more than 8,000,000 now; On Saturday, October 13, 2012, the day after her death, the video had more than 9,000 comments Metro UK reported (http://metro.co.uk/2012/10/13/bullied-teen-amanda-todd-made-youtube-video-before-suicide-599773/), as of August 8, 2013, the number is up 187.408, still counting . . .

[2] Christina, N.G. (2012) "Bullied Teen Leaves Behind Chilling YouTube Video", October 12, *ABC News.*

[3] Hislop, R. (2012). "After Her Suicide, Bullies Continue to Haunt Amanda Todd's Memory Page." October 15, *Global Grind.*

the cyber-bullying of Amanda Todd and expressing their deepest condolences to Amanda Todd's family and friends.[4]

The cyber-bullying continued after her death because it is as cost neutral to bully as it is to sympathize and the cascade mechanisms are the same when based on social proof. New social media can't block human propensities to do deeds good and bad but apparently only reinforce already existing tendencies—infostorms again. The new social media are also lopsided in certain ways, the consequences of which remain to be seen. "Todding" is just the beginning, but for Amanda Todd it was the end.

2.6   The Frailty of Ignorance

Even though pluralistic ignorance is a widespread phenomenon, sometimes having tragic or at least unfortunate collective consequences, the phenomenon still has a weak point. From H.C. Andersen's *The Emperor's New Clothes,* we know that the circle of collective ignorance may be broken by a credible source of information—in this case a small child—pointing out the actual circumstances, which is allowed to circulate to everyone in low voices:

– "But the Emperor has nothing at all on!" said a little child.
– "Listen to the voice of innocence!" exclaimed his father; and what the child had said was whispered from one to another.

If it's true that children and drunks always speak the truth, it means that once the child has released the truth about the emperor's naked self, it's hard to hold back. It happens because everyone suddenly comes to know that everyone else also knows, and what one already had good reason to believe! Thereby the pluralistic ignorance is undermined, since it's precisely erroneous information of others' information which both constitutes the pluralistic ignorance's focal point and the Achilles' heel. Or, if but one student is courageous enough to admit that today's homework in *Sein und Zeit* verged on the incomprehensible, there are generally suddenly more lining up to publicly announce their similar difficulties.

The frailty of collective ignorance has recently been demonstrated in a theorem (Hendricks 2010). This theorem states the relationship between the knowledge *one* person, say a, possesses about a given proposition p, and the ignorance about the same proposition p for every other person u member of a given group of unknowing agents.

Somewhat simplified, the theorem reveals that the child in *The Emperor's New Clothes* (under special circumstances which have no significance here) may transfer knowledge of the emperor having no clothes covering his body to all of those who are in doubt or ignorant about this matter. This means that the collective ignorance may be fought with knowledge transmissibility and general enlightenment from just one single person. In more detail the theorem says that if:

---

[4] Clorox Issues Statement in Response to Amanda Todd Tragedy. The Clorox Company, October 15, 2012: http://investors.thecloroxcompany.com/releasedetail.cfm?releaseid = 713467, accessed August 15, 2013.

1. It is true for all persons u that they are ignorant about proposition p, and
2. After it has been publicly announced that one person a knows p, and that p therefore is the case, then it is true that,
3. After it has been publicly announced that a has knowledge of p, all ignorant persons u will gain knowledge of p if they make use of the same method as a to gain knowledge of p.

If the shop assistant in Computer City, now referred to as a, had decided to acquire more knowledge concerning the computer details, and it became publicly known amongst all colleagues u that he possessed this knowledge, then this knowledge may be transferred to the remaining employees using the same method (presumably by reading the product specifications from the manufacturer) as the shop assistant a had used in order to acquire knowledge of the clock frequency on the bus. Hence, everyone acquires more knowledge, including the customer who asks. That's a good thing. It is exactly for this reason that there are qualified shop assistants in shops, train personnel on stations, lawyers, advisors etc. It might sound trivial, but it demonstrates with desirable clarity the frailty of pluralistic ignorance, and how from time to time, it may be worthwhile listening to experts and widely read people.

The ignorance *wouldn't* necessarily be dissolved if the 'enlightened' person a mentioned in the theorem was merely *informed* of p, but didn't actually have *knowledge* of p. One may in principle be informed of something which is in fact false, and then it's possible that falseness would spread amongst the ignorant persons rather than truth. This would be of no help against the collective ignorance, which under such circumstances would simply, in addition, be supplied with more false beliefs.

Knowledge can't on the other hand be false, because then you wouldn't *know,* even though you may very well believe, assume or even be informed of something. Since Plato, it's exactly this characteristic which is one of the crucial differences between believing, assuming or being informed, and actually knowing. When a knows p, it follows that p is true and then according to the theorem it's truth, which is promulgated amongst the ignorant people, whereby ignorance is lifted. Ignorance may only be dissolved by knowledge. Information is not enough to lift the spell.

If one first realizes these features of pluralistic ignorance, one also sees the similarity between this information phenomenon and bubbles in the financial market—a financial bubble may be conceived as *The Emperor's New Clothes* phenomenon. When the bubble is at its peak, it's sufficient that just one great credible financial player or investor starts doubting the stocks' real value. Subsequently the bubble collapses, as a result of the contentiously self-perpetuating sale of the stock in question, which follows in the wake of the announcement (Hendricks and Lundorff Rasmussen 2012).[5]

Such financial bubbles have been exhaustively studied by the financier and billionaire George Soros in a line of books, where he has moreover argued against

---

[5] Pluralistic ignorance is now reported regularly all over the map of science and society. Recently management and organizational studies have shown how pluralistic ignorance is a prevalent phenomenon in board rooms, on executive commitees, at sales meetings etc. (Halbesleben and Buckley 2004).

market fundamentalism. The blind faith in the notion of the completely free and unregulated market being a self-sustaining and self-regulating mechanism that can solve both economic and social problems—and doubtless also weld under water, shell shrimps and babysit—is to blame for a large share of the world's current economic, social, cultural and even religious difficulties (Soros 2007). More on market fundamentalism and bubbles further one.

Pluralistic ignorance and the danger of manipulation are caused by each person lacking sufficient information, and thus observes others in the hope of becoming wise enough to deliberate, decide or act correctly—looking for social proof. The potential manipulation is rooted in insufficient information. It may meanwhile also go in the other direction. The individual has enough information *per se*, but disregards his own information attempting to follow the same decisions as everyone else—and once again inferring the wrong thing. Too much information plus social proof is as bad as too little information with social proof. The information phenomenon arising in this case is however different, and has a different name. It's called an *informational cascade*.

2.7 Air France, Delta Airlines and Terminals

John F. Kennedy Airport in New York City is a humongous airport with tons of people, airlines, terminals and planes to be coordinated in accordance with the right time and place. Some years ago Air France entered a collaborative agreement with Delta Airlines operating the route between JFK and Paris' Charles de Gaulle. At some point this meant that a plane from Air France might be fitted with a flight-number from Delta Airlines. The problem occurs when Delta Airlines normally fly from JFK terminal 2, while Air France typically fly from JFK terminal 1. What do you do? Check-in at terminal 1 or 2, when it's an Air France plane with a Delta Airlines flight-number?

According to our home printed tickets it said terminal 1. All the people we spoke to on the airport terminal train, however, thought this was a mistake, and that it should say terminal 2. The reasoning was this: "Since it's a Delta Airlines flight number, it naturally refers to departures with Delta Airlines". "Delta Airlines keeps to the enormous and notorious terminal 2. Therefore you have to go to terminal 2". When several other passengers further said that they also were headed towards terminal 2 to catch the same flight, it seemed sensible to follow suit, in spite of our authorized home print saying terminal 1. What we didn't know was that we had just become two more pieces in a rolling *informational cascade*.

An informational cascade is a phenomenon, which may easily occur when a number of people doubt the sufficiency of their own information, and subsequently observes others' preceding decisions and actions in the hope that it can lessen the doubt. This course of action then leads to each individual frequently making the rational choice of following in their predecessors' footsteps, independently of their own preceding information. The underlying rationale is: *If all other sensible people choose to do so, it must be the right thing to do.* Seeing many make the same choice may thus be sufficient testimony to undermine each individual's own decision or judgment of the situation.

To return to the story, we ended up somewhere in between. The following day at 06.30 AM we were sitting in Paris Charles de Gaulle with sore legs from not having enough legroom and with the feeling that it was a hundred years since we had flown from New York. We did manage to catch our Air France flight, but it wasn't from terminal 2, as everyone in the terminal train would have had us believe. No, our Air France flight departed from terminal 1, precisely as our personal authorized print originally had prescribed. The feeling of being idiots had as tough a time subsiding as the soreness in our legs, as well as the hangover from the adrenalin rush which had just managed to ensure that we made it on board the flight from JFK.

The possibility of an informational cascade dawned on us just as we stood at the check-in in terminal 2. All those we had asked had Delta-2-beliefs. The quality of information from our print from home, which stipulated an Air France-1-belief, was in return another matter. Even though we had *most reason* to follow the Delta-2-belief due to social proof, we actually had *another* and *better reason* to follow the Air France-1-belief. Luckily for our fellow travelers, informational cascades can, just like pluralistic ignorance, be rather fragile.

2.8 Amazon and Sex and the City

If one begins to scrutinize everyday life, it quickly becomes apparent that information cascades are highly prevalent phenomena. They cause certain restaurants—bad as well as good—to suddenly become popular and impossible to get a table at. They control the key trends in the sale of new cars. They set the agenda for where we think it's good to live, and what price we are willing to sell our house at. And then they are also to blame for stocks being able to sell again and again, at a continually rising price, without it in anyway reflecting the underlying value of the goods, product or corporation. Informational cascades are at work in all these situations. The problem is though, that eyeing others' actions may apparently be a sensible short cut when you have to compensate for your own ignorance.

Informational cascades are extremely powerful tools, if one knows how to control them. If you can manipulate, undermine or completely remove public signals, so that real knowledge isn't advertised, there is free rein for misleading information to spread through with the domino-effect that characterizes informational cascades.

A telling example of *manipulation of a public signal* with the purpose of creating an informational cascade was when the two management gurus Michael Tracy and Fred Wiersema secretly bought 50,000 copies of their own book *The Discipline of Market Leaders: Choose Your Customers, Narrow Your Focus, Dominate Your Market* from the American bookshops used to generate *The New York Times*' bestseller list.[6] Despite bad, or at least mediocre, reviews, the book managed to make it onto the bestseller list due to the 50,000 copies bought in what may be considered a somewhat clandestine fashion. Here the book would keep afloat for a long time without further interference from the authors, since management aspirants bought the book in the belief that its place on the bestseller list naturally reflected its quality.

Another example is from the summer of 2007, when the blockbuster *Sex and the City: The Movie* was all the rage.[7] During the movie the main character, Carrie Bradshaw, reads a book entitled *Love Letters of Great Men*. Following the release of the movie every fan of the movie and series searched for the book on Amazon—and searched in vain. The book didn't exist, well, not at the time, and fans instead started purchasing the book having the closest wording to the title, *Love Letters of Great Men and Women*. Despite being aware of this, Amazon apparently did little to prevent their search-engine from linking this trifling dissertation from 1924 with a knockout offer on the movie's soundtrack. On top of that there was a reference to literature on *Sex and the City* when doing a search for the book. The information cascade was rolling, so why interfere with the free choice of humans to simply buy what they want? Thereby searching fans were just further reinforced in their erroneous belief. Ultimately it resulted in the dissertation making it to number 134 on Amazon's chart—the undisputed greatest success for this kind of literature to date.

The market was accordingly swift and efficient in optimizing. As it turns out, the book's obscure author C.H. Charles had ceased a long time ago, and with him any potential copyright. The month following the movie's release, no less than three different bestseller versions of the book were published, now with new covers and an abridged title matching the book in the movie: *Love Letters of Great Men*. It's therefore true that the free market is probably the most efficient mechanism in coordinating supply and demand, even in an information market—at least as long as the quality of the information in question is flouted (Hansen and Hendricks 2007).

The above provides two examples of how informational cascades may turn out to be extremely powerful instruments if controlled in such a way as to manipulate public signals, so false information is spread instead of true knowledge. But slugs always leave tracks. The trouble with the manipulative approach is that it leaves traces, which may be tracked by the public, and the subsequent spreading of knowledge may block cascades on the move. This isn't always convenient. It may therefore be better—as long as one has the power—to undermine or completely remove the possibility of registering public signals.

---

[6] Bloomberg Businessweek, "Did Dirty Tricks Create a Best Seller?", August 6, 1995: http://www.businessweek.com/stories/1995-08-06/did-dirty-tricks-create-a-best-seller, accessed August 16, 2013 and Bloomberg Businessweek, "The Unmasking of a Best Seller: Chapter 2", August 13, 1995: http://www.businessweek.com/stories/1995-08-13/the-unmasking-of-a-best-seller-chapter-2, accessed August 16, 2013.

[7] The Associated Press, June 10, 2008: http://www.today.com/id/25083812/ns/today-sex_and_the_city_on_today/t/love-book-sex-city-doesnt-exist/#.UhG7y1Mt2X1, accessed August 19, 2013.

2.9   The Structure of Cascades

It was an article by the sociologist Sushil Bikchandani and the economists David Hirschleifer and Ivo Welch (1998), which put informational cascades in a broader perspective and placed the information phenomenon at the center of scientific attention for sociologists, economists, psychologists and later also philosophers. To better understand the information phenomenon and sharpen the ability to recognize it when it appears for real, it is important to dwell on its underlying logical structure (Hansen et al. 2013). Note that the underlying logical structure is similar to the one generating bystander-effects and one may actually effortlessly move back and forth between the two models exchanging a few modules on the way.

Crudely, the structure underlying informational cascades consists of:

1. A set of rational agents that act sequentially.
2. A set of options between which the agents can choose.
3. A preference order on the outcome of each choice.

The decision is made under uncertainty in the sense that no agent knows which action leads to the jointly preferred outcome. That there is a jointly preferred outcome is essential when it comes to the assumptions made. There is no strategic interaction in the decision problem, so no agent will have an incentive to mislead later agents by choosing contrary to the best of their knowledge. This in turn means that subsequent agents may base their decision not only on their private information, but also on the action of those that act before them. Specifically, the following epistemic assumptions, similar to those governing the bystander-effect case are in order:

1. The underlying structure is known to all agents; the sequence of agents is known to all,
2. Each agent makes a rational decision based on available information, which consists of
    a. A *private signal* about which action will lead to which outcome, which is known to be more often right than it is wrong,
    b. A *public signal* consisting of the string of actions *performed* by the previous agents.
3. Knowledge among the agents that their signals are equally likely to be correct.
4. Knowledge of rationality as described in 2.

In (2b) it's only the *actions*, and not the *signals*, of previous agents that may be observed. Furthermore, one should notice that the sequence of agents is known to all is, in conjunction with 2b., taken to imply that any agent knows what public signal any previous agent received.

A *run* of such a model may be conceived as a line of agents, each waiting to make a decision between a (finite) set of choices (Fig. 2.3). In runs where later agents choose to ignore their private information and act on the information conveyed by previous agents' actions, an *informational cascade* is said to be in effect.

Consider a situation where the agents have to make a binary choice between turning left or turning right at a junction in a maze—or just de-boarding a plane.

* Personal signal
\# Public signal
@ Choice

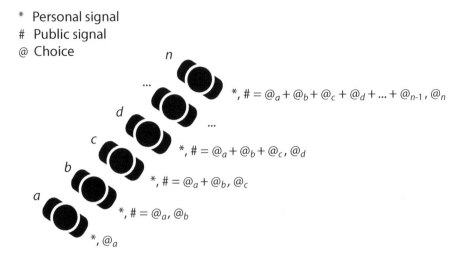

$$*, \# = @_a + @_b + @_c + @_d + \ldots + @_{n-1}, @_n$$

$$*, \# = @_a + @_b + @_c, @_d$$

$$*, \# = @_a + @_b, @_c$$

$$*, \# = @_a, @_b$$

$$*, @_a$$

Fig. 2.3 Simple mechanism for establishing an informational cascade with n persons; each has a personal signal "*" as well as a public signal "\#", and each must make a choice or decision "@". All persons in the sequence, except person a, receive a public signal, which consists of information about what the previous decision-makers have chosen

Before receiving their private signal of *left* or *right*, each agent will be indifferent between the two options. When the first agent receives her private signal, say *left*, she will take this to indicate the correct path out of the maze. Given that she has no further information available, she will follow her private signal, thereby conveying a *left* action to all subsequent agents.

When the second agent must choose, the public signal of an executed *left* action in conjunction with knowledge of rationality may be used to deduce that the first agent's signal was *left*. Two situations may now have occurred: One in which the second agent received the private signal *left*, in which case she should choose to go left, or one where she received the private signal *right*, in which case her available information—a *left* signal from agent 1 and a *right* signal from herself—will suggest opposite responses. Since both signals are known by 2 to be equally likely to be correct, rationality specifies no concrete plan of action. Hence the agent must choose based on some *tie-breaking rule*, e.g., by randomizing, choosing to follow her private signal, etc. For now, assume that the second agent received a *left* signal, and therefore chooses to go left.

The actions of agents 1 and 2 send a public (*left*, *left*) signal to agent 3. Like agent 2, 3 can deduce the private signal of agent 1. Additionally, given suitable assumptions regarding the tie-breaking rule, 3 may also deduce that agent 2 received a *left* signal. As it is known that every private signal is equally likely to be correct, *it now does not matter for her action what signal agent 3 received*. If 3 received a *left* signal, she, too, should choose to go left. If she received a *right* signal, the information extrapolated from the public (*left*, *left*) signal results in left still being more probable than right.

She will therefore choose to ignore her private information and act in accordance with the group behavior. Thereby agent 3 will be the first agent in an informational cascade.

Upon receiving the (*left*, *left*, *left*) action string, agent 4 will also choose to ignore his private signal in case this is *right*, and choose to go left. This action will be chosen on the same basis as 3 made her choice, namely the deduction of the private signals of agents 1 and 2. The fourth agent will, however, not have a stronger reason to go left than agent 3 had, since the choice made by agent 3 is *uninformative* to all subsequent agents. This is a corollary of agent 3 being in cascade: Since 4 knows that 3 is rational and received the public signal (*left*, *left*), 4 can deduce that 3 would have chosen to go left *no matter what private signal she received*. Hence, agent 4 will base his decision only on the choices of the two first agents, and will also be in cascade.[8] Similar considerations apply to all subsequent agents: They will all be in cascade, ignoring both their private information as well as the choices made by previous agents in the cascade.

The model especially clarifies how the very first signals in the sequence are *imperative* for the decision the remaining decisions-makers reach. If the first flight-passengers make a wrong turn after the gate, there's a significant chance that the remaining 300 passengers will blindly follow. Thereby the model also demonstrates that if you can control the initial choices of the sequence, then you can also control or influence the choices and beliefs that the subsequent decision makers adopt—and that happens in spite of their personal assumptions or signals. The same cascading mechanics are partly responsible for creating bubbles in science and opinion bubbles on the web (Cf. Chap. 7) and bubbles on the real-estate market (Hendricks and Rasmussen 2012).

The model further demonstrates that informational cascades may lead people astray. Thereby voters can, by means of readings and exit polls, for instance, gain information about other political positions by observing how others vote. Studies in political dynamics show that people and parties who are quick off the mark with their political positions, messages or proposals are given an inordinately large amount of importance and attention, and exit polls may therefore play a decisive role on election day for those voters who are yet to make up their minds. In the US many states have coordinated their primary election, so that they are placed early on in the election cycle and moreover on the same day—*Super Tuesday*—in order to maximize their influence in relation to the presidential election.

One of the pronounced consequences of informational cascades is, then, that you can make millions of rational people turn *left*, if only the first two do so. This still applies even if the best choice is actually to turn *right*, and if everyone except the first two has real reason to believe that *right* is right. Yet it presupposes that you forget, as was the case in JFK, to distinguish between the *quality* of the information you receive, and only have the *quantity* in mind. When you do that—when an opinion becomes just another opinion on a par with all other opinions—the very *amount of information* becomes a burden hard to escape.

---

[8] The sequence the public signal consists of will have reached what Malcolm Gladwell refers to as a tipping point (Gladwell 2000).

2.10   Status Economics

The cascade mechanisms can explain a number of different societal mechanisms. They shed light on the relationship between informational cascades and social imitation, based on an interesting phenomenon we have witnessed for almost two decades (Frank 2000; Hansen and Hendricks 2007). Simultaneously with economic growth (now gone bust for a while) and advancing individualization, where individuals have devoted themselves to personal development opportunities in terms of recognition, identity, talent and potential and have had the necessary means for this 'self-realization', a convergence has still occurred towards the same trend-things: Four-wheel-drives for urban transportation, expensive watches, high-end apparel, brand labels, designer kitchens and other accessories.

How can it be that everyone is an original individualist and yet they converge on exactly the same things? It's neither original nor independent. The information phenomena under scrutiny all indicate that the explanation is to be found in what happens when we as citizens, consumers or voters don't have perfect information available. The basic thesis is that when you don't possess sufficient information to solve a given problem, then it can be rational to imitate others by way of social proof.

Take for example the market for holiday crime novels. For those of us who are unable to examine the entire market, imitating others' choices solves the problem. We consult the bestseller list and the newspaper reviews as well as family and friends. This can be rather rational, because through imitation you benefit from the information, which others have gained through, sometimes hard, experience depending on the quality of the crime plot. However, it's not a question of a blind imitation process. Imitation is motivated by the problem that needs solving, and one seeks to imitate those who have had success in doing so. But which problem, except for vanity, does fashion solve, and whom should you imitate?

Here publicly private spending has assumed the role that titles and honors had in days of old. It signals acclaim, status and power. These types of signals are naturally social denominations, the meaning of which is only credibly signaled *when each understands that everyone else likewise understands them.* It's like with currency. We only accept the currency we expect others want to receive.

But when the status signal is no longer embedded in a real value, it becomes a question of a self-feeding process where the individual no longer commands any other quality assurance than the status itself. Unlike money, status isn't spent but is simply strengthened when used. *The ones with a reputation therefore end up having a reputation simply because they have a reputation, and celebrities become celebrities for being celebrities.* Just think of the alarmingly high number of reality-show stars produced lately whose only qualification and apparently celebrity impact is that they are like everyone else, and if nothing else, then themselves. But if they can become famous for specifically being themselves, then the rest of us can as well, which is why in principle anyone can become famous for being famous. Status economics may create *status bubbles* (cf. Chap. 7).

By the same process we find the answer to why clothing fashion, car fashion and the rest of the 'superficial' lifestyle products are perfect elements of status economics, as well as why the consumer bonanza celebration of the individual paradoxically arrives in a standard package. Imitation is by its very nature limited to the observable. In a status economy, where there are no other guarantees than the social status itself, successful imitation is thereby the kind of imitation *everyone can see and everyone can understand*—thus the standard packaging.

Meanwhile, honors and titles only have value if an audience, placed in an asymmetrical relation to the bearer of the social symbols, recognizes them. This is exactly why it's so important that we need to hear about VIP-parties in the tabloids, which the audience are, by definition, barred from participating in. For just as the nobility had to acknowledge back in the day, if everyone gains access to the symbols of power, inflation and then worthlessness follow. While everyone converges toward the symbols of power in order to offset the asymmetrical relation, the content of the symbol is constantly changing. This very feature entails a cat-and-mouse chase in the hope of being initiated in the symbol's latest content. The imitation by definition therefore causes inflation of the symbols of power. But where it implies more knowledge as a by-product in a true knowledge society, it just brings along further spending and demands of renewed capital in order to do so in the consumer society. And voila, that's how it all resulted in a jejune economic crisis.

2.11   A Decisive Piece of Information

Just as pluralistic ignorance is fragile, so are informational cascades. Sometimes they are actually more fragile than ignorance. A single piece of new information may be devastating to an otherwise robust behavioral pattern, as long as there is enough juice in the *quality* of the information. On the assumption that humans are rational, it may very well happen that they realize that their current behavior or belief is based on limited or erroneous information. This may force a change of mind or change in behavior to be more congruent to actual circumstances.

Returning to the model, an informational cascade may have a very weak basis, consisting of only the first two actions in the sequence.[9] This is the reason why cascades are often considered fragile: The balance in even a long-running cascade may be upset if actions contrary to the herd behavior are observed. If one allows for agents perfectly informed by their private signals in the model described, it would take *only one agent* to break the cascade.

To see this, assume that the fifth agent in the described left cascade *knows* that she should go right instead of following the herd. She would not ignore her own knowledge, but rather the public signals sent by previous agents, and therefore choose

---

[9] In case no cascade arises in the beginning of the sequence, one will occur in case there are two more agents that choose one action than there are choosing the other. Given that agents assume others' signal to be as likely to be correct as their own, any cascade will commence on an equally weak basis.

to go right. Any subsequent agent may now take 5's action to indicate that 5 had hard information and then simply choose to follow her instead of the cascade. However, even if 5's action is only interpreted as 5 having received a private signal equal in likely correctness to all other agents' private signals, the action is still enough to bust the cascade. For now agent 6 will know that agents 1 and 2 received *left* private signals, that agents 3 and 4 were in a cascade, and that agent 5 received a *right* private signal. Hence, 6 will no longer ignore her private signal. In case this is *left*, she will go left, but if it is *right*, she will choose to act in accordance with the tie-breaking rule. Thereby, agent 6 is no longer in cascade.

If you are able to control the signals received by the first decision-maker in the sequence, you may control what the decision-makers further down the line choose to do, irrespective of their own signals. You may be able to circulate true information with a domino effect, just as you can spread false information in the same way. Truth may therefore be spread at the same speed as falsity. That was exactly how we got everyone over to terminal 1. After all, we only had time to tell those in our *immediate* vicinity—and those who eavesdropped— that we had it all wrong and why. After that, this *one single* piece of information spread like wildfire through the chain of waiting Paris tourists where it finally reached those who we didn't even have time to talk to. The terminal-signal started a chain reaction; everyone changed their beliefs, acted accordingly and made the flight on time.

It's therefore possible that different shock-waves can disturb or ruin the cascade. These are roughly speaking

a. That individuals with true information appear;
b. That new information becomes generally accessible;
c. That shifts occur in the underlying value of approving or rejecting a position, norm or behavioral pattern.

The shock-wave in (a) is akin to the JFK- de Gaulle-terminal-example. Secondly, if it was now publicly announced over the speaker system that "all passengers traveling to Paris Charles de Gaulle with Delta-flight 098, must check-in in terminal 1", it would be an example of the destruction of the cascade with (b). That shifts may occur in the value of approval or rejection, as mentioned in shock-wave (c), is supported by new computer models and simulations in cascade research. In order to understand the basic idea of these simulations we must quickly run through what may be called the true disciples and the disbelievers in a social network.

2.12 True Disciples and Disbelievers

Why do groups from time to time approve of stances or norms that individuals wish had gone to where the sun doesn't shine? A robust and general hypothesis about why humans collectively applaud a stance, position or a norm which individually they don't really care much for is that a fair few actually, by the end of the day, approve of the norm, and exactly for this reason comply with it.

With that said, there may yet be persons who still don't approve of a norm which a group has established. So the group may choose to exercise social pressure on those participants for whom compliance or imitation isn't enough. For a *true* disciple it is not enough that everyone else show up for the right art exhibitions, adorn themselves with the right and very expensive watches, buy the right four-wheel-drives for urban driving and vote for the right party. *If you have to follow suit, you must do it for the right reasons.* On such considerations it's better not to comply with a norm than just to do it for the sake of social, economic, intellectual or cultural gain. Those who comply with the position or the norm for the wrong reasons may be exposed as heathens or deviants. In a social network you therefore roughly have to distinguish between:[10]

- **True disciples:** those who believe or comply with the norm for the right reasons.
- **Disbelievers:** those who either believe or comply with the norm for the wrong reasons, or those who neither believe nor comply at all.

Complying with a norm for the right reasons requires that the behavior in question can be monitored, and that the social pressure is strong and prevalent enough to secure at least silent compliance from disbelievers or deviants. There are numerous examples of such situations—from all sorts of neo-religious movements, to biker gangs and youth gangs. The consequence is often that true disciples simply show contempt for newcomers, who must demonstrate their worth through odd ritual inaugurations, which typically hurt both body and soul.

Transferring the hypothesis from *The Emperor's New Clothes,* this means that those who admire the emperor in the sole wish for social approval ultimately fear that their affectedness will be obvious to everyone else. They thus scout for another way to confirm and signal earnestness. Complying with a populist norm accordingly becomes a cheap, almost free way to advertise sincerity, which supposedly doesn't reflect the opportunist, but on the contrary, the 'true disciple'.

Meanwhile, it's not only the distribution of disciples, deviants and heathens that determines whether cascades are viable. The viability is likewise contingent on which information channels are available to the members of the social network, and moreover how the members are placed purely physically in relation to one another (called the network topology). New computer models and -simulations indicate that cascades of self-perpetuating support for an unpopular norm—for instance ignorance or xenophobia—have a hard time in a completely connected network, where everyone knows everyone and knows their view of the norm or position (Centola et al. 2005). If however the individuals' horizons are limited only to their immediate neighbor or the person standing right next to them, unpopular norms may arise and spread with greater ease. It's predominantly easier to get a cascade of information to spread in a closed office space, where people sit in booths and only have immediate access to the neighbor in the next booth, than in an open office space, where it's easy to venture over to someone in the far corner to get a feel for their view.

---

[10] This is a simplified version of the distinction drawn in Centola, Willer and Macy (2005) and a selective recollection of some of their many pertinent results.

Fig. 2.4 A completely
connected social network,
where everyone has access to
everyone else and knows his
or her respective view or
stance

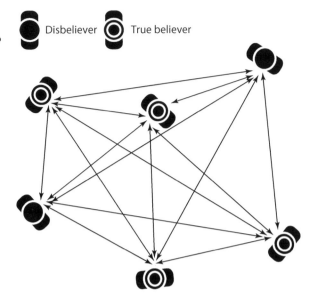

Fig. 2.5 A not completely
connected social network
with a small number of
randomly placed true
believers

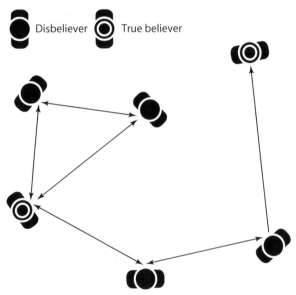

The different scenarios in Figs. 2.4–2.6 graphically describe how access to information between merely disbelievers and true disciples determines whether an information cascade may develop or not in a public space.

In Fig. 2.4 the informational cascade fails, because the disbelievers not complying with an unpopular norm or who don't approve of some particular view have a precise idea of the real extent of public support for the norm amongst the true disciples, since

Fig. 2.6 A social network where random channels between the members

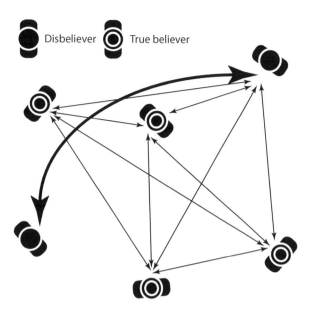

Disbeliever · True believer

everyone knows everyone else's position. In that case the cascade has unfavorable conditions. Open information channels between all members of the social network means that everyone can investigate how great the actual support is for the norm, position or belief, whereby the misinformation about the population distribution is minimized.

Here the cascade fails, inasmuch as the share of true disciples who rely on and comply with the norm doesn't especially digress from the underlying population distribution for which there can be more disbelievers. Thus, there is no great difference to be observed between the true disciples and disbelievers. Furthermore, the limited number of open information channels complicates the acquisition of additional information to confirm how great the support for the norm really is. In Fig. 2.5 the two true disciples in the bottom left and top right corner respectively have no direct access to each other, but only to their immediate neighbors, who by the way are disbelievers.

Finally Fig. 2.6 is a situation where random connections between disbelievers facilitate access to information outside the immediate neighborhood. Accordingly, the disbelievers have access to a more representative picture of the population and thereby a more precise picture of the true state of affairs and the actual prevalence of the norm or position. One can size it up and if the cascade finally hits, one thus has something and someone to resist with.

There is much more to be said about pluralistic ignorance and informational cascades since they also appear to be contingent on the knowledge we collectively possess—called *common knowledge*. Common knowledge may again be used for either good or evil in the battle for conquering the public space. Now, if you are able to conquer public space it's much easier to control pluralistic ignorance, bystanders and informational cascades. We turn to common knowledge in public spaces next.

Chapter 3
Public Space

"But he has nothing on at all," said a little child at last. "Good heavens! Listen to the voice of an innocent child," said the father, and one whispered to the other what the child had said. "But he has nothing on at all," cried at last the whole people.

—The Emperor's New Clothes, H.C. Andersen

3.1 The Invasion of Copenhagen

"The World has Invaded Copenhagen!" So the newspaper headline ran. But the date next to it wasn't 1939 or 1945. Nor had armed soldiers in camouflage-greens walked through the city gates to take up position on every street corner. It was November 2, 2006 in the fairytale country of Denmark—a country known worldwide for its welfare system of equality. But as Shakespeare had already noticed centuries before, something was rotten in the State of Denmark.

The headline was in fact exaggeratedly joyous and referred to the arrival of the international "mega-event" called the MTV-Europe Music Awards. And there seemed to be more than a small unintentional and ironic grain of truth to the journalist's exclamation. While the upper crust of Denmark couldn't stop congratulating themselves on the international "mark of honor" that receipt of this "appointment" amounted to, no one apparently thought much about the implications of voluntarily parking a Trojan horse in the most central public square of the city. For a while all were kings and queens.

As with all events arranged on the principle of the *experience economy*—i.e. public events aimed at the selling of experiences that are either directly or indirectly related to the sale of goods or services—the Music Awards was, behind the scenes, operated, orchestrated and executed by commercial interests. If only for that reason, this should have caused some reflection on the part of the municipality's Cultural Administration before donating more than 1 million USD or 700,000 GPB to support this "cultural event", as the liberal Culture Mayor at that time chose to refer to it. However, if you perceive society's institutions as analogous to corporations—as some modern politicians tend to do (more on this in Chap. 9)—the excuse for not thinking twice was straightforward: The event would in the end be exceptionally good business for the city. Based on previous MTV-Europe Music Awards held in other European capitals and similar experience economic events held in Copenhagen, it was estimated that the city would get in the vicinity of 16 million USD or 10.4 million GPB in returns in terms of visitor spending. Such a profit is by all means hard to ignore.

V. F. Hendricks, P. G. Hansen, *Infostorms*, DOI 10.1007/978-3-319-03832-2_3,

However, things turned for the worse when it suddenly became clear that the Music Awards, including the main event in the Siena-inspired town square in front of the City Hall, was to take place as a *closed party*—or be "exclusive" as it was called in Orwell's Newspeak. Tickets to the symbolic incarnation of *public space* had suddenly fallen under the administration of MTV's commercial collaborators and were to be obtained only by passing auditions or receiving an exclusive invitation. Entry was reserved for people who solely from a commercial perspective qualified as "Very Important Persons": Actors, models, reality-stars, people in the advertising industry, and other such characters who are usually famous merely for being famous. Hence, for one grand night public space was to pose in glory for the rest of the world, in particular our future generations, to see—encircled by fences, checkpoints, and private guards, and without access for the elderly, the ugly, the poor and the stupid.

Fortunately the contradiction in the utterance "Hurrah, I was considered suitable to pay for a ticket to public space!" remained obvious to most citizens. Soon scattered critics could easily advance the simple critique that closed commercial events such as these compromise the idea of *public space* (if not the idea of a public itself)—that is, as they said, it compromised the idea of a physical space to which everyone has access as well as the political and moral guidelines which are derivable from this. The *idea* of 'public space', then, still seemed able—to some extent—to uphold a defense against increasing commercialization of these habitats.

Still, it was no surprise that while the criticism was symbolically acknowledged with a tip of the hat, it was practically ignored and ultimately faded away. When all is said and done, it takes more than intangible ideas to distract from a net profit of 15 million USD. It is not every day that a public space in front of the Town Hall generates so much tangible value. Principles and ideas were thus shelved for a night—and soon it could be announced that Town Hall Square had sold out.

The MTV-Europe Music Awards wasn't the only event of its kind to come to the country. As in the rest of Europe, in the space of just a few years the scenario of a grand-scale experience economy in the name of tourism has become widely accepted in this fairytale country. Copenhagen Fashion Week has probably come to constitute the most extreme example of this development so far. Every 6 months public squares, institutions and buildings such as City Hall and the National Museum close down and are rented out to companies whose products are often made in dimly-lit factories in Bangladesh. Big screens in public squares show beautiful models strolling down catwalks, while massive concert speakers emit polished muzak which is only interrupted when 'the chosen' trendsetters are interviewed and designers preach their commitments. In all its pomp and splendor, few people seem to notice that nowhere in sight are any elderly people or children, nor any wheelchair users, unemployed or otherwise somehow challenged demographics. As a friend of ours visiting from abroad commented, "Everyone seems to be peculiarly fit, young, beautiful, and . . . symmetrical."

In 2010, well into the financial crisis, it seemed that the Fashion Week could get no such thing as too much attention. It was therefore decided that what the world needed most was the longest catwalk ever seen. A 1-mile red carpet was thus laid down through the city. Lying there in the rain, like a fashionable Berlin Wall, it was guarded by fences and private security guards who refused over and over again, and with unconcealed irritation, any citizens who were so (quote) "stupid" as to assume that they were allowed to cross it in order to get home or to work. Senior citizens, people holding real jobs and parents with their kids were forced by compulsory admission to take part in the fashion industry's military parade, since there was literally no way to get around it. However, at this time critics had fallen silent to the numbness of normality. The media had long ago become fully populated with VIP citizens analyzing new trends, alluding to the secrets of celebrity life and pointing out the attraction of the fashionable venues to anyone who dared to doubt.

But perhaps this could have been avoided. Albeit the fences and checkpoints were hopefully not there to stay, critics should have noticed that the ideological pickets surrounding the public space had been moved long ago. For years public space has been increasingly subjected to privatization and commercialization, where every square foot is silently converted into spaces for advertisement and events, whose impact is developed in step with new technologies. There are mounted roller conveyors with background lighting on the stations, above our heads the trains' flat screens are bombarding us with commercials, and by the traffic lights free-sheets are thrust through car windows. On a 'test-drive' walking through Copenhagen to buy flowers, we were obliged to run a hurdle race over a prefabricated first-served offer by a cell phone vendor, pass through a loud street disco erected by a shoe-shop, slalom drive between five shady sign-holders, receive three flyers (two from restaurants and one from a neo-religious movement), firmly refuse four newspaper salesmen, two free-sheets, five employees from the anxiety-industry, three phone salesmen without any sense of personal boundaries, receive eight promotional popsicles and duck a dancing muffin! When we finally made it to the end of the street, we observed that the flower seller had packed his stuff on realizing that an offer shout once in a while could no longer compete with six musicians who had amplified their pan-pipes with a large concert stereo.

Faced with this development, the question that critics should have considered and answered early on was: *What happens when we rent or let out prime spaces and places of democracy to 'experience' economic events?* Nothing, the loud and all too interested people say; after all, the rest of us by and large still have access to public space . . . most of the time. Yet, by considering the societal value of public space this chapter arrives at an alternative answer that is both surprising and complex. What from one perspective looks like good fun and innocent business has from another perspective a price, a price that in the long-run mind you, is divided out very *unevenly* among the *citizens of society.* What we seem to be heading for for is the obvious societal alienation which the horizontally challenged, the ugly, the old, the foreign, the poor and so on experience to an increasing degree, but find extremely hard to put into words. Since what is their problem? Don't they actually still have access to public space on the same terms as everyone else?

This chapter attempts to give them a voice. As it turns out public space isn't really a physical thing. The reason why is to be found in a very special concept travelling the world of microeconomics and logic under the name of *common knowledge.* A closer study of this phenomenon as well as its relation to the value of public space, reveal that the increasing commercialization of this turf may ultimately pose a clear and present danger to democracy.

3.2 Public Is More than the Opposite of Private

Most people recognize that public spaces hold their own very special sort of magical attraction. They are physical voids or watering holes that only come to life by the presence of the crowd. Public space thus has its own nature created like a social fact *sui generis* giving it a special valuable role in everyday societal life. Not only is public space an immediate social arena, wherein each is created though the meeting with the other, as citizen or outcast, as recognized or anonymous, as autonomous individual or merely present as a physical obstacle, but these particular spaces also penetrate a city and its history: They are the scene for the birth of markets, for the public display of power, for executions and revolutions, for obsession and oppression. It's not surprising that the concept of public space is able to break through the concrete shortsightedness of even the unsophisticated and prevailing consumer consciousness as a special pro-social and democratically valuable arena.

But what does this value actually consist in? According to popular opinion and Wikipedia,[1] public space is defined as something physical, rather than social: As a *space that is generally open and accessible to everyone*. But is that really all there is to it? If that was the case, then a roadside in Ohio should be just as precious to the US public as Capitol Hill. Yet it isn't. This means that mere general physical access cannot be all there is to why we (including the advertising industry) attribute such great value to those places and squares that most beautifully cement the idea of public space in our collective consciousness.

Is it then that these spaces are located at the center of the infrastructural networks of the nations and neighborhoods they serve? Isn't it exactly this condition which explains the absurdity of the Chinese government's referral of public demonstrations to remote parks and fields during the Summer Olympics in Beijing, 2008? But again, such a simple physical requirement cannot be the full story either. As the Woodstock festival illustrates, there is nothing that rules out that masses in a remote field can establish their own temporary public space, albeit that it's usually not optimal compared to a central urban square. Hence, although intuitively attractive, centrality isn't a necessary condition for something to qualify as a public space. In fact, recall what strong debilitating consequences historical assembly bans may have on even the most central public space's function. Hence it is evident that centrality is not a *sufficient* condition for a public space either. Altogether this implies that even though *centrality* is a desirable attribute of public spaces, it's not the significant feature.

Historical assembly bans however provide a decisive clue to understanding wherein the function and value of public space lies. The assemblies that such bans seek to prevent are not merely the result of a desire to stand around in groups looking at each other. Even though unthinkable in practice an assembly ban, which consisted in one being banned from *talking* while convening, would be almost as efficient as the classical ban on gathering altogether. In a sense such a ban would indeed undermine the function and value of public space to the same degree as dissolving the

---

[1] Wikipedia: http://en.wikipedia.org/wiki/Public_space, accessed, August 15, 2013.

crowd. As soon as one realizes this, it becomes obvious that the value and function of public spaces is connected to the kind of information and communication they render possible. That is, *a public space is not defined by a range of physical conditions, but by providing an information structure.*

What is so unique and valuable about the information structure that public spaces facilitate? Isn't it just to be understood as all other communication structures, where the information is transferred from one party to another?

3.3   Public Announcements and the Seed of Infinite Knowledge

This question finds a possible answer in a phenomenon that has been studied intensively in formal logic, epistemology and game theory over the past decades: *Common knowledge.*

Common knowledge is as logically complex as it is intuitively simple. Imagine the following scenario: Two guys are sitting in a café drinking hot chocolate with whipped cream. Unbeknownst to them they have both acquired a white whipped cream mustache. Of course, they can't avoid noticing that the other has whipped cream on his upper lip. Yet, neither of them knows that this fact also applies to himself as well. If each of them knew that, they would immediately wipe it off straight away. Yet neither of them does so, because neither of them tells the other so as not to embarrass a friend. After all, had the other one known he had a whipped cream mustache he would obviously have wiped it off at once.

Now the waiter appears with the bill. But when he leaves the table he discreetly smiles at them and says "Are whipped cream mustaches the new trend this season?" in a way that makes it obvious to both gents that both of them now know that one of them must have acquired one. Now this message shouldn't make a big difference. After all both men already knew that one of them—namely, their friend—had acquired this accessory. Nevertheless the waiter's announcement now causes some measure of embarrassment for both guys seconds later and has each straight away reaching for a napkin or shirt sleeve, depending on which is most handy, to wipe away their own whipped cream mustache without saying anything. But how did this happen? *How could they suddenly know what they didn't know before by learning something, which they already knew?*

Somehow the waiter's message enables both men to simultaneously deduce that they themselves have a whipped cream mustache on the upper lip. Yet, it still seems mysterious. The waiter's message reveals nothing more than what the two buddies already knew. Yet, the study of common knowledge and public announcement logic explains how. The fact is that given the public announcement both men know, that they both have heard the message, which implies that they both know, that they both know, that they have heard the message, which again implies that both know that both know... and so on. Accordingly the public message enables *each of them* to reason as follows:

> The waiter has clearly indicated that at least one of us has a whipped cream mustache. Of course I know that, but now he also knows it himself. But hey! Why doesn't he wipe it off then? He would most certainly have done that, if aware of it. But if he isn't aware of it despite the waiter's clear hint, which he definitely heard, it can only be because there is another one in our company who has a whipped cream mustache. But that can only be me! Bummer!

Subsequently they both immediately wipe underneath their nose (unless of course they find it more plausible that their friend actually doesn't mind having a whipped cream mustache).

The reason why the announcement of already known information may have effect is that what the young gentlemen *each* knew has been transformed into *common knowledge* through the waiter's *public* announcement of this knowledge. In other words, that knowledge, which was previously *distributed* between the men, has, through the waiter's message, become 'common' or 'shared' between them, which enables them to deduct completely new knowledge and act accordingly.

What is crucial to notice is that common knowledge isn't just about relevant information being transferred from one person (the waiter) to each of the two listeners (the gents). That is, the crucial component is not that the waiter's announcement transmits the information expressed to each of the men. Instead the decisive element consists in the *public nature* of the waiter's announcement. This public nature provides each of the men with information regarding what their friend knows and does not know. In other words: Each man beforehand thought that their friend didn't know the proposition A: "One of us has a whipped cream mustache"; he now knows that the friend knows this, as well as that the friend knows that he himself knows it, as well as that the friend knows that he knows, that his buddy knows this... and so on for as long as one cares to reason.

To go beyond this example we need to dress up common knowledge in more formal garments. Formally we can write that the waiter's announcement of proposition A (i.e. "one of us has a whipped cream mustache"), elevates A to common knowledge, written $CK(A)$. Yet, it does so relative to the two men and so it is nice to know how the phenomenon of $CK(A)$ relates to them.

To see this we call the two men Irwin and Jack, and refer to them as i and j, respectively. Now, Irwin's knowledge about proposition A prior to the waiter's public announcement is written as $K_i A$ (read as "Irwin knows that A"). Adopting this notation, Irwin and Jack's common knowledge may now be described as follows. From the waiter's public message $\phi!$ about the trendiness of whipped cream mustaches Irwin can deduce A, hence we can say that $K_i A$. However, he already knew that. But the new thing is that given $\phi!$ Irwin can also deduce from this that Jack knows A, that is $K_j A$. This is what he didn't know before $\phi!$. But such a deduction amounts to knowledge itself. From $\phi!$ it follows that Irwin knows that Jack knows A, that is $K_i K_j A$. Given the public nature of $\phi!$ and Irwin recognizing the identity between his and Jack's situation as to what pertains to the waiter's announcement $\phi!$, $\phi!$ may now be observed to work as a seed for what is potentially an infinite chain of knowledge. Why? Because Irwin can infer from $K_i K_j A$ and $\phi!$ That Jack knows this, that is $K_j K_i K_j A$, which now means that Irwin knows this, $K_i K_j K_i K_j A$. In fact, this chain of Irwin knows that Jack knows that Irwin knows that Jack knows may be extended as

long as Irwin cares to reason and the same, of course goes for Jack's situation. This
series may be written:

$$K_i K_j K_i \ldots K_{i/j} A, \text{ if and only if, } CK_{(i,j)}(A)$$

If Irwin knows, that Jack knows, that Irwin knows and so forth, and conversely if
one begins with Jack knows, that Irwin knows, that Jack knows and so on—written
$K_j K_i K_j \ldots K_{i/j} A$—it means that A is common knowledge amongst the two men; and
if something is common knowledge between Irwin and Jack, conveyed by $CK_{(i,j)}(A)$,
it means that Jack knows, that Irwin knows, that Jack knows … etc.

But it is one thing to *define* what common knowledge is. Another is to *explain*
what causes common knowledge; what explains how a given public announcement
or event $\phi!$ may give rise to common knowledge of a proposition A. That is, $\phi!$ must
be incorporated into the model.

In order to do this, start by imagining two people i *and* j, who witness the event
$\phi!$, where a car crashes front first into a tree. It seems obvious that the information
expressed by proposition A: "The driver is injured" becomes common knowledge
$CK_{(i,j)}(A)$. But how does it happen? That is, how does common knowledge come
about between i and j that A, that is, how does $CK_{(i,j)}(A)$, come about?

According to the economists Robin Cubitt and Robert Sugden (2003), the establishment of $CK_{(i,j)}(A)$ may be conceived as follows: First, if $\phi!$ happens, then this
implies that every person i gets to know that $\phi!$, where $\phi!$ represents "the driver has
crashed into a tree". That is:

$$\phi! \rightarrow K_i \phi! \tag{3.1}$$

It then follows that if $\phi!$ happens, then every person furthermore knows that every
other person observing the incident also obtains knowledge that $\phi!$ is the case. This
may be written as:

$$\phi! \rightarrow K_i K_j \phi! \tag{3.2}$$

Well, actually it's natural to assume that if $\phi!$ happens, then it doesn't only follow
that i obtains knowledge of $\phi!$ on the basis of event $\phi!$, and that i obtains knowledge
about, that j knows . It also implies that i knows, that j knows, that i knows, that
happened, and so forth:

$$\phi! \rightarrow K_i K_j K_i \ldots K_{i/j} \phi! \tag{3.3}$$

In other words, then, $\phi!$ is common knowledge, all things being equal; that is, as long
as the witnesses to the accident are minimally rational and assume that all witnesses
to the accident are likewise.

Of course, this still doesn't mean that A: "The driver is perhaps injured" has
become common knowledge. Before this becomes so, it must be assumed that each
witness' previous experience entails that observing $\phi!$ indicates that A is true. That
means that if a witness i observes $\phi!$, then it indicates (written ind_i) to him (given

his previous experience), that proposition A: "The driver is perhaps injured" is true in the given situation. This amounts to:

$$\phi! ind_i A. \tag{3.4}$$

To continue, assume that the witnesses to the accident share a common background of experience, and that they are aware of this. It now follows that when $\phi!$ indicates to i that A, then i also knows, that $\phi!$ indicates A to j that A. This means:

$$K_i(\phi! ind_j A). \tag{3.5}$$

This formula occasions a repetition of itself again and again and again. That is, (3.4) doesn't only entail (3.5). It also entails that "i knows, that j knows, that $\phi!$ indicates A to i", and so forth as long as the agents care to reason it out. In other words:

$$\phi! \rightarrow ind_i A \rightarrow K_i (\phi \, ind_j A) \rightarrow K_i K_j \phi \, (ind_i A) \ldots K_j K_i K_{j \ldots} K_{i/j}(\phi \, ind_i A). \tag{3.6}$$

If it's subsequently conceded that persons i and j are minimally rational, share a common background of knowledge and are both aware of this, all that is indicated as knowledge now becomes knowledge, whereby it follows that:

$$\phi! \rightarrow K_j K_i K_j \ldots K_{i/j} A, \text{ if and only if}, CK_{\{i, j\}}(A). \tag{3.7}$$

Given that persons i and j are rational and share common background knowledge or experience, which among other things includes that they are both rational, then the public event $\phi!$ occasions that proposition A: *"The driver is perhaps injured"* becomes common knowledge among them. Not surprisingly the witnesses of the accident not only deduce that the driver might be injured, whereupon all hurry to the scene to assist; but also that all the other witnesses are likewise aware of this, whereupon everyone expects that all witnesses will hurry to the scene of the accident.

3.4 The Emperor's New Clothes Revisited

Albeit that this analysis may seem like intellectual overkill of an everyday phenomenon that we intuitively understand very well, the extra work soon pays off.

For instance, return to the phenomenon of *pluralistic ignorance*. The above account makes it clear what goes haywire when witnesses to an accident end up in pluralistic ignorance and therefore refrain from coming to the driver's rescue. Just as the driver's sudden confrontation with the tree constitutes a public event that *indicates* to everyone that the driver might have been injured and is in need of assistance, the absence of an immediate reaction from the surrounding witnesses may similarly constitute a public event, which under certain tragic circumstances may *indicate* to everyone that the driver *isn't* in need of any help at all. As long as the witnesses find the latter indication stronger than the first, they will fall into a trap of reasoning which on decisive points is analogous with what the gents at the café experienced:

> If there were need for help, everyone would hasten to the rescue. But there is no one hastening
> to help, so there probably isn't a need for help.

The result of this reasoning pattern, as we now know, may very well end up as a case of the bystander-effect.

Previously it became clear that the orientation act (which boiled down to basics, is responsible for delaying an immediate reaction to an occurring accident) grows with the number of people witnessing the public event. Therefore it's no longer surprising that the danger of pluralistic ignorance also grows with the number of witnesses. The more witnesses, the longer the orientation act takes, and the stronger the indication that the driver isn't actually in need of any help. For the same reason, as previously said, it's better to fall down in a quiet suburban street in Shadyside, Pittsburgh, almost void of people, than to drop in Times Square with oceans of spectators around.

But public announcements or events and the common knowledge phenomena they generate may also work contrary to pluralistic ignorance. That is, they may also lead to the *dissolution* of pluralistic ignorance. Think again of the quote from *The Emperor's New Clothes* this chapter opened with. In the fairytale, the entire court as well as the people has been struck by pluralistic ignorance concerning the emperor's clothes (or rather the lack thereof). However, the common background knowledge, regarding the veracity of drunks and children, leads to the emperor's embarrassing state of undress being recognized as soon as the little child publicly utters: "But, he doesn't have any clothes on!"

This not only shows that common knowledge is closely connected to pluralistic ignorance. It also demonstrates that what is realized as common knowledge is fundamentally decisive for what thoughts great crowds of people conjure up. In reality people tend to ignore drunks and children and thus kings usually go undressed without anybody knowing it.[2] Yet history provides ample evidence that regimes may crumple when citizens take the word of a public gathering—think of what is now referred to as the Arab Spring. Whoever has access to making public announcements in public space may to a substantial extent control or influence what people think of each other and about the world—and thereby also the thoughts they can entertain, and what actions are about to take place.

3.5   The Value and Function of Public Space

The analysis of common knowledge gives a rare insight into public spaces' inherent ability to create architectural frames for public events and signals, and thereby serve as a generator of common knowledge. It is this and not just accessibility that makes them especially valuable to societies. The analysis also pinpoints how it's the basis of the phenomenon of common knowledge—the possibility of transmitting public

---

[2] A series of bystander-effect experiments carried out on the main pedestrian's walk "Strøget" in Copenhagen on July 10, 2013 seem to support the thesis that people systematically are much less prone to assist when a person dressed and acting like a drunk (as opposed to a business woman, an elderly gentleman or a young business man) falls down on the sidewalk (Boensvang et al. 2014).

messages and information—that is eliminated by any sort of assembly ban. Though still accessible such a ban may dissolve a public space as such. This also means that if you hold or gain power over public space, then you also hold the power to control what people think of one another and therefore what they can deduct. This is the real reason why public space is perhaps the closest one can get to an almost physical incarnation of political power.

The link between common knowledge and public space is also witnessed by daily experience. One may follow Michael Chwe (2001) in talking of *the magic circle* (as long as one remembers that magic is on the logic of reasoning). If you start from scratch the magic circle already exists in those situations where only two people communicate face to face. Observing such conversation it is clear how the most fundamental behavioral norm is that participants *look* at each other while talking to each other. The reason why this is so fundamental as well as seeming so natural to us is precisely because we, by looking into each other's eyes instantaneously establish what's spoken of as common knowledge. Focus is to be devoted to the conversation, and every little twitch of facial muscle signals attention and underlines understanding. It's all about common knowledge. Just a split-second's (literally) absentmindedness puts into doubt whether what's been spoken of has been established as common knowledge, and thereby what later on can be presupposed as such. Common attention creates common knowledge, which again establishes a common background of knowledge and experience, which amounts to the fundamental resource for future thought and collective action.

Of course, any kid in kindergarten knows this. They also know that the 'magic circle' isn't limited to two people's exchanges or interactions. Sitting in a circle is the most basic collective human ritual even among these little people. But the magic circle is not only a significant part of any child's social education. It is seemingly also the most fundamental political institution in any society. This has a straightforward logical reason. After all, the circle is the closest one can get to direct eye contact with larger groups of people. It renders it possible for each participant to see that everyone else is attentive. In the magic circle, then, a community is established in the form of common knowledge created through utterances, discussion and the acceptance of public messages and events. On these grounds it's not surprising that one can find the magic circle as a central institution in the management of political power throughout world history. From the great Kivas of the Central American Indians in Pubelo Bonito to the Roman senate, and ultimately to the parliamentary chambers of Western democracies, the magic circle constitutes the basic architectural principle. The circle of seats bordered by a rostrum therefore seems to have become the democratic political power's physical base configuration.

That being so, it is not surprising that various power circles are ultimately subjected to the magic circle, for which only a 'public space' can provide the physical frame. As any democratic or despotic leader is aware, political power always rests on public acceptance—whether speaking of the Middle Ages or the 21st Century, no system has ever survived full-blown public rebellion. Thus the understanding of public space's basic function as a foundation for common knowledge as well as the inherent possibilities for creating information phenomena such as pluralistic ignorance or informational cascades, provides not only the basic concepts for understanding society's fundamental fellow-feeling, but also for the political power ruling on this very basis. As the scientist and philosopher Michael Polanyi very tellingly has described it:

> [...] If in a group of men each believes that all others will obey the commands of a person claiming to be their common superior, all will obey this person as their superior [...][A]ll are forced to obey by the mere supposition of the others' continued obedience (Polyani 1958, p. 224).

So it seems that it is not until we actually realize the complexity of the public space's function, which includes common knowledge, that we understand the real foundation of political power.

Political leaders and despots have always had an intuitive understanding of this exceedingly potent cocktail. Churches usually distort the nature of public gathering so that everyone looks at one and the same person, without being able to look each other in the eye. The royal procession through highways and byways is worth little without an audience, and it's the presence of an audience and not the despot's parade, which forms the procession's pivotal point. For it's precisely through the crowd's presence that the despot cements his power and the subjects' obedience by way of pluralistic ignorance. The festive mob with waving flags doesn't form the surroundings, but is *the* center point for the royal procession, which amounts to the clear public signal of 'broad public support' for the 'festivities', which thus causes opponents to shirk from the dangerous thought of dissent. The festivities surrounding successions are not just an innocent homage, but rather potent forcible means.

It's precisely in this light that one should understand why regimes such as China, Cuba and Iran deploy crowds to publicly mark their support for their rule. Voluntary or not, the crowd's presence still amounts to the powers' physical incarnation, whose size is equal to the challenge which political opponents should be led to believe exists. But it's also in the same light that one must understand why the police in the remaining Western monarchies still perform preventive arrests of any 'bully', whose crime is to wield republican banners to the Queen's driveway; or when the police are requested to keep political opponents away from the ruling party's 'festive' media parade in front of parliament. Roughly speaking, *albeit a festive event, be aware that it might actually be a closed party.*

3.6 The Common Value of Public Space

While the aforementioned examples bear witness to why power circles and prominent citizens value the public space, they yet say nothing about what the value of public spaces consists of for the regular citizen. Luckily whenever police perform 'political-preventive-initiatives' this gives a key clue.

Public space must be understood as a special *information structure* rather than a physical *admission criterion*. Hence it's not surprising when it turns out that public spaces are remarkably sensitive to, and strongly linked with, information phenomena such as pluralistic ignorance. But just as inevitable and necessary as the function of public space is as a political tool of power, this tool only works by leaving the political power to the crowd—*the foundation of democracy*. A ruler's power naturally consists only of the power he or she can invoke, and when this is done through the presence of the crowd, the crowd compose an unstable reactor core with its own dynamics determined by the public space's inherent 'laws of nature'. Hereof the possibility of pluralistic ignorance is but one.

When it actually qualifies as such, public space is the fundamental base for mass democracy by providing an open information structure. With unlimited access to a centrally located public space there arises freedom and equal access for the greatest number of people, to communicate information and views in such a way that they become an inevitable part of society's common consciousness. As many still recall, Chinese students employed exactly this tactic to demand a more participatory democracy during their large-scale demonstrations at Tiananmen Square in 1989. The Chinese regime was naturally well aware of the threat that thousands of unarmed students and workers could present against a comprehensive political and military machine by merely sitting down in the public space. The regime therefore sent soldiers and tanks into the square. But they similarly had to realize that even a single man with two plastic bags in his hands can stop a column of tanks, if only everybody watches, and everyone knows that everyone is watching, everyone knows that everyone knows that everyone is watching and so on. The common value and *raison d'être* of the public space consist hereafter in the opportunity which such spaces give each individual to demonstrate almost infinite powers and knowledge to the society that surrounds them. Again, the Middle Eastern revolutions in the spring of 2011 showcase the same point. Here the mob's annexation of central public spaces and squares has worked as the root that has nurtured rebellion. Modern information technology has furthermore managed to expand this space to such an extent that the scope of common knowledge perhaps accounts for one of the most important differences between the rebellions in Egypt and Syria.

The common value of the communication possibilities, which only public spaces can provide by way of their special information structure, is however not limited to fighting despots and regimes. In modern democracy public spaces play a constant and fundamental democratic lead part in the procurement of reciprocal recognition amongst the citizens, solely by their physical *presence* in these spaces. The simple physical representation in public space of all society's citizens in all their shapes and sizes establishes on its own a public signal, which inscribes itself in our common consciousness. Upper-crust and famous figures, homeless people in cardboard boxes, religious minorities, children playing in parks, elderly people with walkers, school teachers with pupils chasing pigeons, white-collar guys with draught beer, key account managers who flash fancy watches, students with books, hard workers with rugged fists wrapped around a hot dog etc.—all have a right to a place in democratic consciousness: Since if we are not all represented in our common consciousness and common background knowledge, then we have removed the basic prerequisites for the democratic debate, the frames of which are *equality*, *freedom* and *mutual respect*. The common value of the public space is therefore a fundamental value for our democracy, whether speaking of Tiananmen Square, Brandenburger Tor, or the steps of the Lincoln Memorial, which provided the setting for the famous words "I have a dream."

3.7 Techno-Ideological Pickets

We all seem to possess an intuitive or casual understanding of the public space's society-promoting value. Most of us now and again seek out one of society's central squares in order to affirm ourselves by the presence of others. Yet Copenhagen Fashion Week and MTV-Europe Music Awards are just two examples of how new technologies threaten to monopolize the information structures of public space with the purpose of serving those private interests who can afford their services.

Tailored mega-events driven by an economy of experience push to an increasing extent wagons of sponsored nudity, tax deductible marketing parades, big screens and concert speakers into our public streets and squares. Here they now amount to a new type of one-way communication, where a well-defined socio-economic group utilizes the diligent manipulation of public announcements, pluralistic ignorance and informational cascades as the direct tool for profit maximization. It's not merely a question of a financed expropriation and monopolization of the public space, but also a change of its essence. We are no longer being *spoken with*, but *spoken to* in a communication parade that doesn't take note of hecklings or protests (try yelling at a billboard and see what happens). Simultaneously, the mere acceptance of mega-events constitutes a pronounced public signal about which values society should be ruled by. It's a parade of the emperor's new clothes through the public space with an audience that has been robbed of its voice.

Truth be told, it's probably both seductive and striking. But maybe the reason for our love of public squares in the sun-kissed countries of the Mediterranean should be found in exactly the maximum democratic deficit, which the minimal economic profit leaves behind to society when the party is over. The increasing alienation of society's diverse groups cannot be surprising when society's common knowledge is managed by the market interests' *echo chamber*, rather than in the community's *public space.*

But is there really an alternative to the prevailing commercialization of public spaces that is occurring all over the world? It seems there is. In 2007, the world's fourth-largest metropolis and Brazil's largest city, São Paulo, became the first city outside the communist world to put into effect a radical, near-complete ban on outdoor advertising. *Lei Cidade Limpa,* or Clean City Law as it is called, meant the city was stripped of advertising. No Posters. No flyers. No ads on buses. No ads on trains. No Adshels, no 48-sheets, no nothing. The law was an immediate and unexpected success, owing largely to the determination of the city's mayor and the help of key allies amongst the city's elite. Surveys indicate that the measure is extremely popular with the city's residents, with more than 70 % approval. One of the first effects after the introduction of the ban has been reported to be the sudden entry into public consciousness of previously hidden shantytowns and backyard factories with illegal immigrant workers.[3]

---

[3] Harries, D.E. (2007). "São Paulo: A City Without Ads", Adbusters, August 3, 2007: https://www.adbusters.org/magazine/73/Sao_Paulo_A_City_Without_Ads.html, accessed August 4, 2013.

Chapter 4
Wisdom of Choice

> *Democracy cannot succeed unless those who express their*
> *choice are prepared to choose wisely. The real safeguard of*
> *democracy, therefore, is education*

—Franklin D. Roosevelt

4.1 The Invisible Hands of Democracy

However politically incorrect it may be, the "free world" is often regarded as some-what synonymous or co-extensive with the reaches of Western culture and democracy. But the main drivers of Western culture seem no longer to be the freedom of religion, or the freedom of vote. These days the riches of the Western world are more often attributed to our belief in an unbounded competitive market. The freedom of individual choice performs as the fundamental mechanism ensuring optimal arrangements by an invisible hand. At the core of this ideal is a rich and competent consumer, who freely chooses between numerous products imported from all corners of the world. But for many "the freedom of choice" as asserted in the shopping aisle has also become the main template for understanding what our freedom does and ought to amount to politically. Challenge this premise and you are declared a fundamentalist, fascist, or socialist. Still, in this chapter we consider whether *consumer democracy*, and its idea of a constant maximization of the freedom of individual choice, really is the right model to build society upon, or whether it will lead to societies that come to closely resemble shopping centers? We do this by peeling the concept of the freedom of political choice like an onion.

4.2 Positive Freedom

Without further qualification one may peel off the first thin layer of the ideology of the freedom of choice holding that Western riches are due to a unique love and respect for freedom itself as little other than a manifestation of egocentric self-glorification. Should it really be true that Indians, Sudanese, Chileans, Chinese and Japanese don't value liberty? Hardly. Nevertheless, such self-interested diagnostic constructions often go unchallenged. The winners usually claim history, but these days rarely take up the responsibility to even read it.

V. F. Hendricks, P. G. Hansen, *Infostorms*, DOI 10.1007/978-3-319-03832-2_4,
© Springer International Publishing Switzerland 2014

What perhaps *is* distinctive of the Western world is that we not only conceive of the concept of freedom of choice or liberty as the mere *absence of arbitrary exercises of power or constraints*. Totalitarianism and traditionalism may control all aspects of public and private life in very general and non-arbitrary fashions. Instead we demand of liberty that it is also *the freedom to act, and individually choose without the interference of others*. That is, being free means not merely that we aren't forced into a religion or to get married with a particular person. It also means that we can choose our own religion and to whom we want to get married. Thus, expressed by a classical distinction drawn from philosophy, it would be most accurate to say that we not only culturally conceive of liberty in its *negative sense* (the absence of constraints on our actions), but also in its *positive sense* (freedom to personally act on and define our own goals). *Self-determination* would be another word for it. But what is it that is so valuable about self-determination, that we don't merely just consider it as the sacrosanct ideal at the frozen goods counter in supermarkets, but also as the most qualified mechanism for dealing with almost every possible political or economic decision?

An obvious factor is to be found in the psychological experience of dignity and independence often referred to as *autonomy*. This miniscule but crucial difference in our way of experiencing certain of our actions and choices as self-determined is perhaps the main reason why we value the freedom of choice and attribute to this a fundamental value in our lives: The self-determined choice to choose for oneself, what we wish to believe in, who we want to love, who we want to vote for, what books we want to read, what we want for breakfast, and how long we want to be standing in the shower. The sacredness of this kind of choice seems subsequently to follow from the simple consideration that in the end it's such choices, which define who one really is as a person. It's only by being free to make your own choices that you can realize the person you are and the life you want, and simultaneously feel a certain dignity and independence in your actions—no matter how predictable the rest of the world sees you. Self-determination is the cornerstone of individual freedom.

To illustrate, imagine that you are sitting in a restaurant with a friend, spouse or one of your parents. Imagine now that this person knows you so well that he or she can predict exactly what you prefer from the menu. Then compare the situation where you get to order what you want as a starter, entree and dessert yourself, with the situation where your friend, spouse or parent orders for you, without even asking you. Even though the outcome is the same in both situations—you get to eat what you would like from the menu—there is still a significant difference. While the result of the first situation expresses your own independent choice, you are simply passive in the other situation.

Seen from the outside the difference might appear small, well almost dispensable. Seen from the inside it appears so important to most people that they, all other things being equal, and at any one time, would insist on ordering themselves, despite the trouble. Of course, the experienced self-determined choice seems to be the only relevant difference between the two situations. Yet, the infringement of this inner psychological experience of self-determination shows us how intimately entwined this is with our feelings of personal dignity and independence. This becomes particularly apparent during the teenage years. Parents watch in despair as they realize that their child is beginning to choose the opposite of whatever they suggest, simply because the value of expressing the independence linked to self-determined choice is more important than what is actually chosen. This *admittance* is however generally also the first step toward the *acknowledgement* of the young person as an independent and grown up adult. It seems only natural then, that this experience should be protected and kept in moral regard. But why should it also be regarded as politically relevant?

4.3   The Relevance of Self-Determination

Now, one can reasonably object that if the free choice must be acknowledged as a fundamental value to society, it requires more substance than just the psychological experience of independence and self-determination over those choices regarding only you. Western culture and its fundamental institutions of democracy and the free market ought to amount to more than just a common cultural teenage rebellion.

However, we all seem to know the convincingly simple answer to this: The politically relevant value of individual freedom of choice consists by way of the fact that in almost every conceivable situation one is usually the one who *knows* best what one actually prefers or wants. Individual choice is efficient, for who could make the right decision for you better than *you*? That's probably also why the waiter, for the sake of safety, would usually ask you what you prefer from the menu if others should try to decide for you. Just to make sure. Even our best friends or spouses through many years may easily be mistaken in their judgement—let alone our parents—who are however excused, since they once actually did know us so well and perhaps still do.

Individual freedom of choice easily presents itself intuitively as by far the best way, if one aims at treating the individual as an adult and responsible human with the right to define, achieve and realize personal wishes and goals. If someone were to object, one can effortlessly illustrate the point by putting self-determined choice in sharp contrast to the far less efficient paternalistic measure, where one always leaves it to others to decide on ones behalf. In fact, this contrasting is what is ritually performed whenever someone questions the legitimacy of exerting individual choice in *any* given context.

Still, notice the tendency in the public debate to assume efficiency of individual choice for any situation, however far removed it may be from the simple and straightforward one of ordering food in a restaurant or choosing the brand of detergent in the shopping mall. Thus individual choice has to a steady extent been ascribed the role of the ideal instrument (well, almost a panacea) not only to obtain efficiency, but also quality and innovation in much more complex social relations, where the results of the individual's actions depend on the actions of other people involved. In a sense one may observe that in recent years the idea of freedom of individual choice has achieved a peculiar religious status, which has swept through the Western political world like a rhetorical tsunami that threatens to destroy anybody who stands in its way. Recognizing this, the political reaction across the board has been to go with the flow and open the gates of almost any institution, except democratic vote, to the forces of market fundamentalism. The basic assumption seems to be that nothing better can represent democratic opinion and collective action than the invisible hands of consumer democracy.

In the absence of a real political challenge to this notion, "freedom fighters" with former experience from blitz-war against supercilious arbiters of taste and knowledge, non-existing weapons of mass destruction in foreign countries and other straw men, have easily been able to secure the continuing advancement of individual choice and its individualization of institutions. Citizens have applauded the freedom of individual choice of school for their kids, the freedom of individual choice of hospitals, freedom of individual choice of education and so on, without paying a second thought to the consequences. Finally, we have also obligingly learned to use a new political lingo in which words such as 'welfare service', 'quality insurance', 'innovation', 'supplier' and 'consumer' have substituted the earlier vocabulary where central concepts were 'care', 'respect', 'sincerity', 'helper' and 'fellow citizen'.

But perhaps the time has come to stop and think twice. The big question is, whether the consequences of the onward march of consumer democracy are as straightforward when it comes to the complex social relations which make up society. The next pages reveal why there are no guarantees of efficiency, quality and collective optimality automatically following in the wake of the distinctive version of the freedom of choice that today like a spectre haunts Europe and the Western world. Looking at an array of simple examples we show how the simple notion of the freedom of individual choice, even under perfect information, may easily lead to bad consequences for ourselves as well as our fellow citizens. In the end, this raises the question of whether the cult of individual choice has at all understood what the politically relevant version of freedom is, or whether they aren't just up to selling us a special incapacitated version of this in order to get regulation removed that serves the 1 %.

4.4 Political Freedom and Individual Choice

It's by no means uncommon to hear even educated journalists formulate political freedom or just "freedom" in terms of the sheer ability to individually choose freely from amongst whatever options are currently available or considered possible candidates of choice, i.e. as consumer democracy. "Shouldn't one let people decide for themselves—aren't they capable of assuming their own responsibility, and do they not have the right to choose freely?" has become the typical rant whenever the discussion turns to the politics of society. The main idea behind this reaction is that:

Individual choice = political freedom

On the basis of the previous chapters, it is remarkable how rarely it is added that real political freedom must not only include the right to individually choose freely, but at least also some amount of relevant *information*. Political freedom only seems to make actual sense—one only seems to have a real *good reason* to pursue and defend the freedom of choice—provided that one possesses, if not perfect information, then at least sufficient relevant information in the choice situation to *actually being able to achieve that which one is aiming at achieving with ones choice*. When we recognize such a deficit of information we usually follow one of two strategies. We may either (1) ask someone else to choose, or we may (2) ask or look to someone else or seek out further information. Here we are pursuing the path of self-determination where the value of political freedom cannot merely be defined as being allowed to choose freely amongst whatever options are available in the status quo—we at least have to include some measure of information.

Not any measure of information will do. Think of *pluralistic ignorance* and *informational cascades*. It's evident here how information can get us to make what appears to us to be a free choice, but with very unfortunate consequences as a result—both in an individual and collective sense. Hence the students choose, dead against their self-interest, to remain silent rather than ask questions, because they didn't possess the relevant information concerning their fellow students' trouble with the homework. We similarly saw how book buyers on Amazon were driven to seek out books which didn't exist, and how tourists can voluntarily go straight into expensive and bad tourist traps when it comes to choosing restaurants in a foreign city. For free individual choice to have a political relevancy it therefore presupposes a sufficient amount of relevant information based on real cognition. Hence, neither the ideal of individual choice, nor that of political freedom is satisfied by the mere freedom to choose in a positive sense.

But does

Individual choice + information = political freedom?

There seems to be some sense to this. Didn't the previous chapters show us exactly, that it's manipulation by way of information or just the lack thereof, which makes us vulnerable to, say, swindlers with special economic interests? If one places a book on top of the bestseller list, it becomes a bestseller; if it becomes a bestseller and you manage to "keep the children quiet", people easily continue to believe that the emperor is still wearing clothes, instead of believing even the direct evidence provided by their very own eyes. But if we instead had *perfect* or just *sufficient relevant information*—preferably as *common knowledge*—about the relevant sales figures on the book market or what other people actually think when they see the emperor walk past, would the problem pretty much be solved? At least, given that we add that what each individual can choose between is offered on a competitive market this seems what most people are beginning to believe: Once we have the freedom of individual choice in this sense, it trivially follows that our individual as well as our collective interests will be realized without much difficulty.

4.5 Walking the Dog at Night

There is a problem with any claim to the effect that freedom of individual choice, conceived as choosing freely with sufficient information, should trivially induce efficiency, enhanced quality and other celebrated effects. This may be illustrated by a simple study of dog pooh on the street.

A couple of years ago one of us (Pelle) became the 'lucky' owner of a genuine Chihuahua—and a particularly small one at that. The best part of this acquisition turned out to be the contentious amusement it has caused Vincent since then. For instance, it quickly turned out that the dog was so peculiarly small that it could only be walked at night, if one wanted to avoid those curious dog owners who, "lie in wait behind every street corner, with the desire to bond over ringworms, chew toys and mating potential" as the unhappy owner usually voices it. The resulting nightly walks with the creature have however proved to have certain advantages. It has especially allowed for the study of those aspects of human behaviour which are unable to stand the light of day. One of our favourite objects of study has thus become other dog owners and the dilemma they are faced with on the street when Rex, King, Bella etc. has answered the call of nature: Should one as the owner take care of the problem or leave it to its own devices?

If we approach this problem systematically, the dog owner's immediate dilemma consists of the following choice: (a)"Pick up" or (b) "leave it". When this decision is viewed in isolation, any dog owner prefers, like any normal creature, to perform (b), rather than (a). If this were not the case nature would have created dogs such that they could pick up after themselves. To schematically model the predicament one may thus construct the following model, where the number next to the action represents the *subjective utility* the action has to the individual dog owner *relative* to the alternative. While higher numerical values exemplify that the decision maker prefers the associated values relative to the choice represented with a lower value, these numbers have no further meaning on their own.

Dog owner 1	»pick up«	1
	»leave it«	2

Game matrix (4.1)

In modern decision theory one uses models such as this to study simple choices by prediction and reconstruction. The model illustrates the fact that, all things equal, dog owner 1 prefers to perform the action "leave it", rather than the alternative "pick up". Now, of course, this is only so because 'the model builder' has reconstructed the values so these accord with observations. Hence there is so far not much won by the construction of boxes and figures.

But if we now add to this dog owner 1's valuation of the *possible outcomes*, which occur when his actions are combined with actions performed by other dog owners, things become a little more interesting. The result of doing so may be illustrated by expanding the simple decision model above to the *game matrix* given below.

Dog owner 2

		»pick up«	»leave it«
Dog owner 1	»pick up«	1,1	-1,2
	»leave it«	2,-1	0,0

Game matrix (4.2)

The notion of a game matrix is taken from the branch of decision theory called *game theory,* where one is concerned precisely with decisions in complex social relations. In this particular game there are two *players,* dog owner 1 and dog owner 2, respectively. The two players are faced with identical decisions—that is, the choice between "pick up" and "leave it". The possible combinations of these decisions pave the way for four different *possible outcomes,* represented by the four cells in the matrix. Every outcome has its own cell, wherein it's represented by two numerical values, separated by a comma. The first numerical value in a given outcome represents dog owner 1's personal valuation of this outcome relative to this player's valuation of the other possible outcomes, while the other numerical value represents dog owner 2's valuation of this outcome, again relative to her evaluation of other alternative outcomes of her actions. The game matrix may now be used to exemplify how each dog owner's individual choice determines a final outcome that is both tragic and ironic at the same time.

To see why, notice that from the game matrix it becomes apparent that the two dog owners prefer the outcome where they both choose to "pick up" (valued by both to have a value of 1), compared to the outcome where they both choose "leave it", (valued by both to have a value of 0). This reflects the fact that dog owners, just like all other sensible people, prefer clean sidewalks rather than walking in "a load of crap". But how can this be, when the observable fact in most towns is that the sidewalks by and large form an utter museum of droppings from all possible dog species?

The answer to this question is found by looking closer at the model to see how the dog owners' individual desires and actions interact so as to produce the tragic outcome. To gain precision we make sure that the model applies to the real world where there are usually more than two dog owners in a given neighborhood. In this situation it still holds that they all share the same predicament. This can be incorporated into the model by assuming any given dog owner to take up the role of dog owner 1, while the role of 'dog owner 2' is set to represent the aggregate decision of the remaining dog owners in the entire neighborhood. Thus if we assume that all the other dog owners choose to "pick up", this corresponds to the generic 'dog owner 2' choosing to pick up, where after we can study the choice-predicament faced in this situation by any given dog owner in terms of 'dog owner 1'.

So what does dog owner 1 do, provided he is sensible and assuming that he expects everybody else to choose "pick up"? If we look closer, it becomes apparent that dog owner 1 is now faced with the decision between "picking up" and "leaving it" in the situation where dog owner 2 (all other dog owners) have chosen to "pick up". To study dog owner 1's predicament we only need to focus on the game's first *column* and identify the action which is related to the best result for him. Hereby the choice actually becomes identical with the first simple game matrix (4.1), where it's recalled, any sensible person would prefer to "leave it". Viewed accordingly the case remains the same since one single dropping doesn't ruin the possibility of being able to walk comfortably down the street after all, and simultaneously one avoids the prickly experience of picking up 'the hot potato'. So that's our answer: Given that he expects everybody else to "pick up", the individual dog owner will prefer to "leave it". Of course, the problem is that everyone shares this predicament—everyone is dog owner 1 from his or her perspective. Hence, we have, *if it is expected that everyone else chooses to "pick up" after his or her dog, then each individual dog owner prefers to "leave it"*.

Next take a look at the situation where each individual dog owner (i.e. dog owner 1) expects everyone else (i.e. dog owner 2) to choose "leave it". This means that in studying dog owner 1's predicament we can now focus on the second column of the game. However, the game matrix once again shows us that under these circumstances dog owner 1 still prefers the action "leave it" to "pick up"! After all, the reasoning goes, a single "pick up" won't save the tragic condition of sidewalks anyway, and favouring accordingly one again avoids the uncomfortable and demanding experience associated with "pick up". (In fact, it may be noticed that if all others choose the action "leave it", while you choose the action "pick up", then you end up with the worst possible outcome, where you have to pick up as well as be forced to walk around in all the other dog owners' 'guilty conscience'—therefore the negative value -1 for this outcome.)

Finally, revert to the point that each individual dog owner from his or her own perspective is "dog owner 1". This ultimately means that the tragic and ironic conclusion follows: No matter what all dog owners are expected to do—"pick up" or "leave it"—each individual dog owner prefers to "leave it". Tragically and ironic since this leads to the outcome of the game, which *all* dog owners find less satisfying than the outcome where *all* choose to "pick up". An answer to the question why the sidewalks remain in their faecal condition in spite of our individual preferences to the contrary and our freedom to choose is therefore to be found in the way our actions interact when situations are complex and involve others. In this situation then, individual freedom of choice doesn't lead to the preferred collective outcome.

4.6   Individual Choice and Climate Negotiations

If you think that it's only dog owners who are subject to this logic, you would have to think twice. The same problem is evidenced in relation to trash, chewing gum and especially cigarette butts. If everyone else chooses to make a mess of the street, it's all the same whether one adds an extra butt, a piece of chewing gum or an empty bakery bag. If everyone on the other hand chooses to behave 'nicely', it still doesn't make any real difference if one personally opts for the easy way. Even though we in principle don't want to be walking around in a load of rubbish, it unfortunately often ends up this way.

What is even worse, however, is that this logic isn't restricted to the sidewalks. Consider the rolling climate catastrophe, the principal cause of which is our extreme emission of CO_2. There is little doubt that we would all prefer a world where we bite the bullet and cut down dramatically on the behaviour, which leads to climate change, rather than pay the piper for a world of migration, famine and wars, which is what we have ahead of us if the emissions aren't checked.[1]

As the international negotiations at the COP conferences have shown, we do have a serious problem on our hands. Even when we gather the world's most brilliant political minds (and some that are not so brilliant), it's apparently more or less impossible for them to coordinate on solutions that are relatively easy to identify. However, it's not necessarily that politicians are ignorant or cynical. As the dog owner's dilemma shows, the problem in attempting to reach such agreements is that when people begin reasoning—whether European, American, Chinese, or Indian— they all fall victim to the same tragic logic as the dog owners:

> We're not going to do anything if they are not. If everyone else makes a mess, we would be stupid to constrain ourselves. . . but if no one else messes, it can't after all cause any harm that one continues to make a mess.

Since this tragic conclusion is identical for all parties, it's no wonder that many politicians' main involvement in the climate crisis has proved to be a creative trade and book-keeping of CO_2-quotas, combined with the obvious abandonment of responsibility and steady dreams of speedy technological advances. The ideological child is a weird one, allowing you to lie in the bubble-bath of a hotel suite watching the news, thinking that it's CO_2-neutral because the hotel chain paid some money to someone in Nigeria.

But what does this say about the freedom of individual choice conceived as being able to choose freely plus perfect information as a candidate for political freedom? Well, our first conclusion must be that when the dog owners' refrain from employing their bag, it appears to be a question of choosing freely under perfect information. Their actions are voluntary, performed with a complete overview of the choices in the situation, as well as real information regarding the resulting consequences. You do choose freely whether you want to pick up after yourself, or leave it be—and you are also well aware that provided you fail to pick up, then the likelihood of someone else doing it is, well negligible.

The second conclusion is that the ability to choose freely given the relevant information far from implies a fulfilment of our common interests in a given situation. As the ideologies concocted around the climate negotiations show, we prefer to cook up absurd stories to repress this fact. There is no guarantee attached to individual choice even under favourable circumstances that prevents us ending up in the seemingly paradoxical situation where we as a result of our unconstrained freedom, but against *our will,* are in a load of crap and water up to the neck—that's a bad mix.

---

[1] In fact, given that a lot of the behaviour that causes our enormous CO_2-emissions is so immaterial that it doesn't have any direct influence on our quality of life—perhaps the contrary—it shouldn't be that difficult.

Putting these two points together, we get that individual choice understood as choosing freely given the right information in *simple situations* does not guarantee that we achieve what we want in the more complex social relations and institutions that comprise societies and the human world as such.

4.7   Market Competition and Tour De France

But maybe we haven't done individual choice full justice. Its standard application, especially in Europe, is not in the context of climate crisis, but rather in arguments for "free choice schemes" instead of state regulation in the "supply" of "welfare services" to "active and informed citizens" on a *competitive market.*

In fact, the dog owner's dilemma might as well be used as an example in favour of the freedom of individual choice given that one remembers to include the notion of a competitive market. In other words, one can imagine the recipe of political freedom retained as:

Individual choice + information + competitive market = political freedom

Individual choice is allowed to defend itself as a means to delivering efficiency, quality, and collective optimality if let loose on a free and competitive market. In this model, the players aren't citizens, dog owners or politicians; they are companies that compete to deliver to these markets.

To see why, picture two corporations which compete freely on market terms, rather than two dog owners hiding in the shadows. A classic argument for how free competition leads to efficiency is that even though companies prefer to maximize profit, competition nevertheless leads to the lowest prices possible for the consumer.

Thus revert to the game matrix, substitute the two dog owners for two corporations, and relabel the choice to "pick up" with "excess price" and "leave it" with "cut-price". As even a quick glance at this new game matrix reveals, both corporations prefer the situation where both charge "excess price" rather than "cut-price" for their services. Luckily for the consumer, free competition in this game means that the outcome will be services at a "cut-price". Even if the two companies should agree upon maintaining artificially high prices, against consumer interests, both companies would swiftly have an interest in going back on their part of the agreement. For as soon as one of the corporations charges an "excess price", the other one would get away with lots of extra customers, and thereby conquer market shares, by dumping their prices to "cut-price". In short, individual choice in the context of a competitive market can work to the advantage of the consumer or citizen.

The only problem with this interpretation is just that the truth is rarely that simple. Still, it's not so complicated that any family guy, who has spent most of his summer vacation indoors watching *Tour de France*, can see how the corporations' dilemma described above doesn't adequately represent the free competitive market.

These days Tour de France is primarily associated with two things. One is the small breakaway group, which heroically fights across sponsor teams on the mountain slopes in order to keep the peloton behind. The other is the recurring doping scandals, which have shown that the Chicken, the Hen, the Eagle and whatever else they are called, each have had more additives through their veins while working the pedals than a middle-sized poultry stock from Iowa.

If we begin with the heroic breakaway group, we come to realize that the situation here is parallel in certain respects with the dog owner's dilemma as well. In the first place, the situation is such that when a breakaway group has gotten far enough away from the peloton, each rider is faced with the choice to either "cooperate" or "freewheel". Secondly, it's true of any serious breakaway group that each rider prefers the situation where *everyone* "cooperates" by pulling their load, rather than the situation where *everyone* is "freewheeling". And lastly, it also unfortunately applies that if all other riders choose to "cooperate", then each rider would, all things being equal, prefer to be "freewheeling", while only a fool would choose to "cooperate", as long as all the others in the group chose to be "freewheeling". In other words, the riders' decision problem is seemingly identical with the dog owners' dilemma: Each individual prefers to act in such a way that the common interest is undermined by individual choices—yet to keep the peloton away, they have to solve this problem of cooperation and often do. Time and time again breakaway groups may be observed to cooperate on the verge of what is physically impossible just up until the finish line.

From a game theoretical point of view, such cooperation between riders immediately appears as both beautiful and paradoxical. We are after all dealing with players who are in direct competition who suddenly cooperate almost as immaculately as the finest clockwork. This doesn't make sense when looking at the game matrix. So when coming across examples like this, it must be granted that there is something wrong with the model with respect to what it's supposed to represent.

So what's wrong? Some would say game theory itself. Examples such as this, contradicting the conclusion of the dog owner's dilemma, have often been used as a launch pad to try and reject the game theoretical approach to the study of human behaviour. There are many people, even within the world of social science, who don't like the idea that human behaviour to a certain extent follows a mathematical recipe. A classic objection is therefore not surprisingly, that human cooperation emanates from those kinds of unselfish motives that we all love to ascribe ourselves but cannot capture well in mathematics. Thus, perhaps the reason for the observed cooperation in the breakaway group should be recovered from man's fundamental ability to be able to act altruistically, or what about a particular human joy for cooperation?

Now, there is no doubt that both motives actually exist to a certain degree, and they obviously have in common that they directly undermine an otherwise competitive situation. When it comes to *Tour de France*, one loves and admires the scenes in the Alps maybe most of all because the cooperation across teams inspires a fundamental hope, respect and admiration within us—that is, when we see humans in unity rise above their conditions and constraints. Yet one should keep in mind that the Tour-riders neither seem to cooperate because of the emotional joy of cooperation or because of pure brotherliness and altruism. While there is hardly any doubt of them personally feeling joy and admiration for each other by the very cooperation, it cannot be ignored that many of them put various needles in their bodies as soon as the others look away. In that respect, the Tour-riders are neither better nor worse humans than the rest of us.

Instead, the explanation for the observed pattern of cooperation and clue to correct the game theoretical model should probably be found in two elements that separate the breakaway from the manner in which we have studied the dog owner's dilemma so far. First, the situation of cooperation in *Tour de France* differs from the dog owners' dilemma in that it is performed in a context, where the riders time and again must choose between performing their part of the "cooperation" or remain to "freewheel" when their turn arrives in the shift cycle. The riders play the dog owner's dilemma with each other again and again during the day. Second, the riders can constantly detect whether there is anyone "freewheeling" when they were in fact supposed to pull and in such cases threaten to dissolve the cooperation and let the breakaway collapse. These two elements combined mean that it's no longer a case of a solitary game of the dog owner's dilemma, where the participants can leave the scene of the crime under cover of darkness. Instead it's a case of a *repeated dilemma*, where there is always the possibility of sanctions—even though these sanctions in the breakaway punish the collective rather than the individual. This possibility of sanctions combined with the game's repetitive nature is what can make "cooperation" the most sensible action for each rider.

Freedom of individual choice shows us why dog owners are far more inclined to "pick up" after King during daylight than after nightfall. Daylight enables mutual surveillance and a large repertoire of possible sanctions, ranging from disapproving looks to supercilious comments. When such social sanctions of each "freewheeler" are added to the dog owner's dilemma, it in many cases entails a change of what actions the parties involved prefer.

More importantly it shows why individual choice, given full information and a competitive environment doesn't *guarantee* the best solution for the citizen understood as a consumer. Corporations on the free market can easily keep an eye on whether others attempt dumping prices, and accordingly threaten with a price war. Figuratively speaking, then, there is nothing about competition, which guarantees that the players of the free market's *Tour de France* don't slot together in beautiful mechanical teamwork, selling their services at "excess price" dead against the consumers' interests. It's of course illegal for corporations to agree on artificially high prices or outlining market shares. If one however looks closer at the example above pertaining to the breakaway group, one soon realizes that explicit agreements are by no means needed in order to establish cooperation between experienced riders. The same goes for the market; all it takes is one knowing each other's interests, rehearsing the dilemma daily and both monitoring each other's prices.

At the end of the day, there is good reason to be sceptical of a naïve version of the freedom of individual choice that unequivocally praises this as being the ideal instrument to secure efficiency and quality in the supply of welfare services in the public sector. Social interaction between people in society is a complex matter and may turn out very differently—both for individuals and groups—depending on circumstances that go well beyond the mere presence of free individual choice based on relevant information. This is true whether you think of the citizen as the quarterback or the receiver in the game of political freedom. But what then: Is there an alternative conception of politically relevant freedom, or are we bound to accept that citizens will sometimes lose some of their "freedom of choice", as it is often claimed, when government and public institutions opt for something other than free choice systems on the premises of competition; when it comes to the so-called supply of welfare services? Or as we began the chapter by asking: Is the individual consumer's ability to choose freely the best template for understanding what political freedom amounts to?

4.8 Ulysses and the Song of the Sirens

Most people are probably familiar with the story of Ulysses and the sirens. In this story Ulysses faced the challenge of his ship having to sail past the sirens whose beautiful singing made seamen jump overboard straight into certain ocean death. Yet, Ulysses wanted to hear them singing. Ultimately he solved the problem by letting his men tie him to the mast, so he could listen to the sirens' spellbinding song without simultaneously throwing himself overboard. By doing so, Ulysses freed himself from the trammels of the situation. (As for his men, Ulysses solved the problem by having them stuff their ears with wax.)

Should we now believe the ritual response of consumer democracy to Ulysses' actions, that Ulysses by using this strategy subjected himself to incapacitation and lost his freedom in a politically relevant sense? Hardly. It's correct that Ulysses renounced the freedom of choice while he was listening to the song of the sirens, but that was merely the result of his enactment of another kind of freedom of choice—a free choice based on wisdom, sufficient knowledge, and insight applied in a larger perspective. Ulysses thereby saved himself from the depths of the ocean, even though it must have been his greatest wish throughout the duration of the song. This story points to a version of political freedom which is about more than the ability to choose freely at any time, even if given the right information in a competitive environment. This version of freedom incorporates wisdom of choice and the ability to transcend constraints collectively. This version is particularly crucial when it comes to the situations one chooses to place oneself in, and thereby also the choices one must make, when the music starts to play. It's here the real value in the Western democracy's celebration of political freedom and the respect of individual opinion lies: *The freedom to personally be a part in choosing the arrangement of the complex society in which we must perform our daily trivial choices*. Given this insight, there can hardly be any doubt that the recent naïve idea of political freedom and choice as individual choice maximization has misled many people into believing a selective truth, through its highly selective perspective on what the politically relevant concept of their freedom consists in.

But if so misleading, then why have we swallowed the idea hook, line and sinker? Returning to our point of departure, we recall the psychological experience of independence and control associated with plain freedom of individual choice. Linked with the idea that individual choice, plus the right information and competition, automatically results in societal efficiency and quality, a dangerous cocktail emerges, where we voluntarily rush after being able to choose for ourselves, regardless of whether we have sufficient information, and regardless of whether our choices actually result in the realization of what we intend. Instead we act blindly, by solely focusing on the possibility of the next false psychological fix of control and independence in the complex social relations which constitute our social reality. Maybe it will dawn on us too late that the cult of "freedom of individual choice" has sold us an incapacitated version of political freedom, which has severed us from the real freedom of choice: The kind of freedom, the most important ability of which is offering a political perspective that gives us the power over our own societal destiny.

Chapter 5
Freaky Framing

> *To a considerable degree the art of politics in a democracy is the art of determining which issue dimensions are of major interest to the public or can be made salient in order to win public support*

> —Maxwell E. McCombs & Donald L. Shaw

5.1 Trafficking in Frames

Some time ago, TV was running an ad for an insurance company that glowingly announced some product offering 170 % "guarantee". This offer is apparently significantly better than the fixed deposit. Instinctively one would assume that 170 % gives you a package with your money back and an additional 70 % on top. However, the specific insurance plan the company advertised had the presumably innocent condition effectively requiring the policyholder to keep the investment for 10 years before seeing anything like the so-called "guarantee" ante up. A little arithmetic will soon enough tell you that 70 % over 10 years is precisely the same as a quarterly compounded fixed deposit interest of 5.3 %. Honestly, this deal would be hard for any conscientious banker to offer.

Similarly, the citizens in and around the medium size Northern European capitol of Copenhagen were not too long ago faced with the choice of whether they wanted:

1. A *toll ring*, where anyone who ventures into the city by car must pay a toll, which ultimately just constitutes another tax to the municipality and state

or

2. An *environmental ring*, implicating a fee for every motorist travelling into the city, which may relieve the environmental strain and reduce pollution in and around the capital.

Same difference, no difference between (1) and (2). Where (1) emphasizes the negatives regarding a traffic encroachment against vehicles in the capital, which is just another tax burden for the citizens, (2) accentuates the positives in contributing through a fee, in order to achieve a better environment and fewer cars in the city's townscape.

The choice you are faced with in both cases is the same—toll or environmental ring still amounts to money out of your pocket while driving into the city and 70 %

V. F. Hendricks, P. G. Hansen, *Infostorms,* DOI 10.1007/978-3-319-03832-2_5,
© Springer International Publishing Switzerland 2014

over 10 years is in the end equivalent to a quarterly compounded fixed deposit interest of 5.3 % as the insurance ad would have it but not say. The only difference is the perspective or the *frame* in which the choices are formulated. Where such frames affect people's decisions independently of what is actually being chosen or decided between, this is referred to as *framing effects.*

In principle, the perspective shouldn't have any influence on one's decision, especially since the perspective doesn't pertain to the essence of what is being chosen between. A rational person should only be concerned with what is really being decided between, not the frames as such. A toll ring or an environmental ring either way involves paying money to the authorities for motorized private vehicles or company trucks in the city. It should be of no consequence whether one refers to the payment in positive or negative terms.

A *frame* is a specific way of presenting, or a particular perspective on, the information required to reach a decision or make a choice. Then

a framing effect occurs when two logically equivalent (but not transparently equivalent) statements of a problem lead decision makers to choose different options (Rabin 1998, p. 36).

The effect works by two choices that are actually the same, but frame the case in different ways, making people prefer one alternative over and above the other. It is not transparent for the parties that the alternatives represent the same decision problem. They are therefore inclined to attach significance to the frame itself. It is a well-known phenomenon that people have a tendency to make both systematically faulty decisions as well as downright inconsistent choices, solely dependent on whether the frame focuses on positive or negative features of the decision problem.

5.2   Choosing Between Life and Death

Any question or questionnaire, and every opinion poll must naturally be worded before it can be answered. In turn the danger of framing effects is always present. In a now legendary experiment, the Nobel Prize Laureates in Economics from 2002, Amos Tversky and Daniel Kahneman, demonstrated how different framings influence otherwise sensible people's choices, even when the decision problem is mainly formulated in objective numbers and concerns something as important as life and death (Tversky and Kahenman 1981).

In the experiment a group of participants were asked to make a choice between two different procedures (**A**) and (**B**) for the treatment of 600 patients with a terminal but hypothetical illness. The only thing the subjects were told pertaining to procedures was that:

- Treatment **A** will save 200 human lives.
- Treatment **B** with a one-third probability that 600 people will be saved, and a two-thirds probability no one will be saved.

Treatment (**A**) and (**B**) have mathematically the same result. Nevertheless 72 % of the respondents chose (**A**), while only 28 % chose (**B**).

Another respondent group was presented with the same scenario, but now with the consequences described from a different perspective—that is, with the focus on the death rather than the survival rate. Thus the choice was now between:

- Treatment **C**, where 400 people will die.
- Treatment **D** with a one-third probability that nobody will die, and a two-third probability that 600 people will suffer a fatal end.

Faced with these choices the respondents supremely preferred treatment (**D**) with 78 % above 22 % to (**C**).

The difference in preferred choice in these identical decision problems testifies to the influence of framing effects. It is not only a question of framing effects having strengthened or toned-down the participant's preferred choice—no, the preferred choice has actually been turned upside down.

The explanation is to be found in the fact that while the wording of the first decision problem emphasizes a positive frame focusing on the number of lives to be saved, the wording of the second decision problem accentuates a negative frame, where the focus is on death and destruction. If you don't take the wording into account, procedures (**A**) and (**C**) have exactly the same consequence: If 200 people are saved from the terminal illness, 400 will die. The same similarity is in play between treatments (**B**) and (**D**), which likewise have the same statistical consequence. So if you prefer (**A**) over (**B**) in the first scenario, you also ought to prefer (**C**) over (**D**) in the second scenario. Treatment (**A**) is nevertheless the preferred choice in the first scenario, while (**C**) is disfavoured to (**D**) in the second scenario.

Once having discovered framing effects, it can't come as a surprise that one also finds them as favoured tools of management consultants, commercial agents, politicians and spin-doctors. With the right frame it seems that you can get people to believe and do pretty much anything. Take for example something as fundamental to our social order as the just distribution of societal boons. Important decisions are reached about complex social relations in a hotchpotch of key performance indicators, legal measures and projected consequences all appropriately dispersed over different social groups. Such a jumble leaves the door wide open to framing effects.

To illustrate, Nobel Prize Laureate in Economics from 2005, Thomas C. Schelling, once confronted his students with the following question (Schelling 1981):

> Would you be for or against a taxation rule, which gives larger tax exemptions to rich than to poor parents?

Such a taxation rule was not taken on too kindly by most of the students. Schelling accordingly rephrased his question:

> Assume a taxation law which targets couples with children, and which penalizes childless couples. Should this taxation penalty be greater to the poor than the rich?

The students now reversed their preferences even though the two scenarios describe the exact same consequences.

5.3   Framing a Problem

A framing effect depends on a *decision problem*. But how is a given frame connected to the decision problem, and what determinant is in play for which frame to chose?

A decision problem consists of the following ingredients:

1. The possibilities, actions and measures to be chosen between.
2. The possible consequences or outcomes of these actions or measures.
3. A specification of the circumstances or conditional probabilities, which connect outcomes to actions.
4. The preferences of the decision maker pertaining to outcomes and conditions.

To describe a decision problem on this basis may seem a rather trivial affair, since (1)–(4) signify a range of conditions which may be fairly objectively determined.

Framing effects may however occur since actions or measures, as well as their possible consequences, must necessarily be described and explained to the decision maker. Hence a decision frame is placed onto a decision problem. The very frame then shapes the decision maker's *own* understanding of possible actions and outcomes as well as the relationship between these two. The frame, which a decision maker relies on, is partially determined by the formulation or exact wording of the decision problem, and partially fixed by the norms, habits and personal characteristics which just so happen to fit the decision maker, interest group or band of voters in question.

Consider a public health care system in which the waiting lists for certain operations have been running tediously long for some time. Patients as well as the general public are running as tired of this as the waiting lists are running long (Hansen and Hendricks 2011). The administration in power may choose to stick with the current unpopular arrangement or try to introduce a treatment guarantee for patients using private hospitals to help bring down the waiting lists. These options and the decision problem coming along may be formulated in more than one way. The actions included in the decision problem may be framed as a choice between:

(a.1) *status quo* or provisionally channel government funds to the private healthcare system,

or

(a.2) *status quo* or bankroll the private hospitals.

The same goes for the wording of the possible outcomes or consequences of (a.1.) and (a.2). These may respectively be described such

(b.1) that the private healthcare service proves helpful in reducing waiting lists and secures the treatment guarantee provided by the state,

(b.2) that one gilds the private hospitals, and takes the public healthcare system hostage.

Finally, actions (a.1.), (a.2) and outcomes (b.1.), (b.2) are linked to each other such that:

(c.1) if you choose (a.1), then you pay homage to the idea that the public sector rests on private enterprising as stated in (b.1.).

(c.2) if you choose (a.2), then the state systematically and deliberately pays too much for the services offered by the private sector (b.2).

The frames are determined by the decision makers' *own* interpretation of the actions, outcomes and relationship between these two scenarios. That's exactly the reason why right-wing politicians, at least in Europe, assuming they allow some sort of government mingling, are in favour of decision frames (a.1), (b.1), (c.1.), while the left-wing sticks to the decision frame given by (a.2.), (b.2) and (c.2.). Politicians tend to use frames on a regular basis, even though the net result of the political proposals, undertakings and initiatives is the same whether one chooses one or the other. Therefore the focal point of political debate often enough becomes which frame best or most adequately describes the decision problem, rather than the objective measures and possible consequences of the problem at hand. No wonder that voters are often confused, and think that politicians talk at cross-purposes.

Is it at all possible to reach any sort of agreement about the correct frames for one and the same decision problem? Figuring frames is like estimating the relative height of mountains, skyscrapers or aerial masts jammed up next to each other. Reason dictates that under normal circumstances, the relative height of two mountains or skyscrapers cannot change or even reverse just because one changes vantage point. Driving from one mountain towards another and experiencing that the former, which at the beginning seemed the tallest, gradually becomes smaller and smaller, while the latter becomes bigger and bigger, we don't conclude that it's the size of the mountain that changes, but rather that it's our own perspective that shifts. The same fundamental idea governs rational decision theory since our preferences with respect to consequences and thereby the actions leading to them ought not change, or turn upside-down, merely because we change perspective, i.e. decision frame. In other words, preferences of rational agents shouldn't be a function of changes in the decision frame.

Framing effects demonstrate that changes in perspective often end up turning the perceived relative height of a mountain, skyscraper or aerial mast, as well as the relative desirability of choice possibilities in matters of state and democracy, up-side down. So maybe humans aren't rational or maybe "everything is relative"; the penultimate point of many a coffee table political discussion before closing? While we can ask a construction engineer or a geographer to measure the objective difference in height between the buildings or the mountains, no such objective measuring unit for our individual preferences, independently of the formulated decision problem, exists.

Real life decision makers are indispensably dependent on the very wording of the decision problems presented to them. This doesn't mean that our preferences are helter-skelter and thereby that one formulation is as good as the next. It does mean that a given decision problem should be formulated as unbiased and coherently as possible, without any manipulative attempt while describing the decision problem. But when political debate becomes a "war for votes", and neither experts nor journalists want to keep a tight rein on the discussion, no wonder that coherence and unbiasedness may go down the drain.

5.4   Risky Insurance

People may support a labour-political initiative resulting in 90 % of the work-force being in business, but on the other hand refuse the exact same political measure when presented as 10 % unemployment. Furthermore, framing effects show how choice works between risky alternatives. Often

1. People prefer *risk-averse* alternatives, when outcomes are framed by what may be gained (for instance saving lives or earning money), but
2. Change to *risk-seeking* alternatives, when the exact same outcomes are framed by what one stands to lose (for instance dying or losing money).

This tendency is similarly evident in Tversky and Kahneman's original experiment: They found

1. That 72 % of the respondents chose treatment **A**, which is the *risk-averse* alternative, where 200 human lives are saved,
2. While 28 % of the trial subjects chose treatment **B**, the *risk-seeking* alternative since there is a one-third probability of saving 600 people and a two-thirds probability that none will be saved.

In the other trial, only 22 % of the test subjects opted for **C**, with 400 casualties for sure, while 78 % chose treatment **D** with a one-third probability that nobody would die, and a two-third probability that 600 people would suffer a fatal end. It's thought-provoking that treatments **A** and **C** are equivalent; 400/600 dying is actually the same as 200/600 staying alive. The treatment programs **D** and **B** are similarly equivalent. In short, preferences with respect to identical treatment programs change by more than 50 % due to relatively minor changes in the decision problem framing.

The provision of different portfolios of risk-reducing measures, all of which cost big bucks, is something that insurance companies have turned into a lucrative business. Framing effects, you see, are closely linked to how *certain* or *pseudo-certain* one feels with respect to the alternatives chosen between. *A sure gain is preferred to probable gain, while a probable loss is preferred to certain loss.* Precisely this phenomenon is something insurance companies are inclined to speculate in when designing insurance policies.

A policy which for instance, covers cases of fire but not cases of floods may either be read as complete protection against a particular risk, i.e. fire, or as reduction of the general risk of property damage (Tversky and Kahenman 1981). Insurance apparently appears more appealing to potential policy holders when presented as downright elimination of risk, rather than when laid out as a reduction of risk. Since no protective measures or actions exist which will cover all the risks humans are exposed to, or expose themselves to, the insurance business is based on probabilities. The fundamental reliance on probabilities is concealed by well-chosen wording in interminable insurance policies and clever advertisement campaigns stressing full protection against clearly identified damages and abominations. The sense of certainty and security the choice of words induce are to a fair extent hocus-pocus produced by framing effects. Typically we don't buy insurance policies because we believe we are out of luck, we buy them to feel on the safe side—just in case. The problem is just that one may manipulate the anxiety factor by the way in which the information regarding the possible risk is presented.

5.5 Fumbles in Frames

The constant threat from framing effects is a troublesome issue, which raises a fundamental question about the role of citizens and whether and when their advice should be sought in public affairs. If citizens' preferences are influenced to such an extent by arbitrary changes in the decision frames, then politicians or opinion-formers should neither take notice nor adapt their political initiatives to what the public opinion, as expressed in polls, votes and all sorts of different undertakings, amounts to.

For instance, if people approve of a particular political proposal, when described in light of freedom of speech, but simultaneously renounce the very same when formulated in reference to affronting others on religious or cultural grounds, the public opinion when so influenced becomes a useless tool in forming public policy and regulation. Some have gone as far as to say that framing effects

> raise radical doubts about democracy itself . . . How can even sincere democratic representatives respond correctly to public opinion when empirical evidence of it appears to be so malleable, so vulnerable to framing effects? (Entman 1993, p. 57).

If framing effects really control people's preferences, dispositions and decisions and thus are constant and very robust phenomena, democracy is facing a severe problem. Given framing effects, one may be able to manipulate democratic processes and important democratic decisions, solely by means of information presentation, and that undoubtedly makes democracy as a whole a rather fragile entity.

But perhaps things are not quite as bad as they appear, and the potential influence of framing effects on sundry democratic matters is maybe slightly over-stated and -rated. New research indicates that even though framing effects are neither irrelevant nor insignificant, their importance is overestimated, both when it comes to the consequences of the theory of rational choice, the democratic situation, human's every day choices and preferred stances about this and that. Framing effects should rather be seen as contingent phenomena, which may be reduced or plainly eliminated under different circumstances, where one adheres to *credible guidance*, and where humans consult to obtain more information.

If one pays it a second thought, there's something peculiar about the experimental conditions under which the classical framing effects are registered. In a typical experiment, a trial group is put to solving a problem, which is stated in a particular frame (for instance death or unemployment), while another cadre of test subjects are asked to solve a logically equivalent problem formulated in another frame (for instance life or employment). The framing effects occur when the two groups give voice to very different preferences. The results of the classical experiments are impressive, since they range from economic to social decision problems, have great variation in populations of respondents and can be reproduced again and again.

But participants are asked to make decisions under conditions where they are neither in social contact nor enter a social context. That's hardly consistent with the circumstances under which we form our preferences every day or make decisions. Before you decide on one or the other, you often discuss it with others, and you attempt to gather more information if you are in doubt about the decision frame's wording of the alternatives. By and large, you interact with your surroundings in different ways to qualify the basis for your decisions. The reverse is not true of the participants in the original experiments, who are asked to reach a decision without access to information, communication or guidance and that naturally increases the likelihood of framing effects. In most social, political and economic contexts we are part of in everyday life, there is often the possibility of interpersonal contact and exchange of information, which potentially makes the framing effects less widespread. This also shows how important active participation is for democratic processes. The classic election meeting with a panel debate separates itself decisively from the modern TV-duel by providing possibilities for reducing the framing effects.

5.6 Information in New Frames

The classic hypothesis about the framing phenomena holds to the idea that framing effects are resistant to further guiding information, and that human preferences therefore remain the same in spite of such information. A more recent hypothesis is meanwhile, that when people receive advice and guidance, they'll use them independently of whatever frame they are subjected to. If this hypothesis is correct, it means that preferences may be based on adequate, systematic information. People can thus base their preferences on their beliefs as well as credible signals, whereby their preferences will no longer be singularly dependent on the way the decision problem is worded (Druckman 2001a). If that's the case preferences, which are based on systematic application of credible information, make much more sense as a tool in the political decision process, public policy and societal administration.

If one again pictures a situation where people must decide on the measure employed in combating a hypothetical deadly disease, but where political parties are now allowed to provide advice and counselling, the situation revolving around framing effects in the modified experiment looks somewhat different.

Political scientist James Druckman, building on Tversky and Kahneman's experiments from 1981 has demonstrated this feature experimentally. In a new setting, test subjects may choose between a risk-reducing alternative:

- Treatment **A1**, which saves 200 human lives, approved by the **Democrats,**

and a risk-seeking alternative **D1:**

- Treatment **D1**, in which there is a one-third probability of saving 600, and a two-third probability that no one is saved, approved by the **Republicans** (Druckman 2001b, p. 68).

The two treatments are again equivalent. According to the experimental findings, framing effects still play a substantial role. In this trial 77 % of the respondents chose the risk-reducing alternative, when presented with a frame for what they stood to gain. On the other hand 56 % chose a risk-reducing alternative, when placed in the same frame for what they stood to lose. But it could simultaneously be observed that the party support of a treatment problem reduced the framing effects. Where 56 % of the respondents chose a risk-reducing alternative, when supported by the Democrats, only 24 % did the same when the treatment program didn't have any party support at all.

Another suggestive result originates from a situation where the Republicans support a risk-reducing alternative, while the Democrats approve of a risk-seeking one. Now, party support has a pronounced impact, which almost drives the framing effects into oblivion. Of the respondents, 31 % chose the risk-reducing alternative, when framed by what one stood to gain. A measly 16 % went for a risk-reducing alternative, when framed by what one stood to lose. Turning to gain frames only 31 % of the democratic supporters sought the risk-reducing Republican program. This is in contrast to the 70 %, when the same alternative was cast as program **A1**, supported by the Democrats.

What about the independent voters, who neither support one or the other party? Presumably the alternatives supported by parties one personally doesn't support don't matter to independent decision-makers, since one doesn't consider partisan advice and guidance as credible. So the framing effects apparently have solid influence on independent voter's decisions across the systematically varied decision problems. If one for instance compares the Tversky-Kahneman-experiment with Druckman's more recent results, it becomes evident that 45 % of the independent voters reverse their preferences depending on the frame, and moreover, that the framing effects pretty much remain in effect independently of party support. Party endorsements are not really part of reducing framing effects for independent voters.

5.7 The Art of Framing Democracy

The situation with framing effects is perhaps not as hopeless as initially feared. Maybe one can put more stock in public opinion in the sense that it is more than a mere reflection of arbitrary and possibly manipulated formulations of decision problems.

Outside the lab, humans have access to information and listen to advice and guidance from others, especially in situations where their preferences aren't clear. This is of importance to the political decision process, as well as public policy, regulation and administration. The quality of public opinion improves when people have access to information, advice and guidance from familiar, credible sources.

This naturally begs the question, what do credible sources and reliably acquired information actually amount to? There may apparently be situations where political stances of parties with respect to a particular decision problem may amount to sufficient credible information. It presupposes however, that the parties involved are not direct stakeholders in the decision problem given. Combating hypothetical diseases is not an extremely heated issue politically, but of course it doesn't take much before it does become politically controversial. A treatment guarantee for patients in a public and private setting is clearly a hot potato, which recent years of political battle, especially in Europe, have testified to with non-disclosures, lies and threats of impeachment. In such situations it may be so-so with the credible information from political quarters.

The question of choosing sources of information is linked to an information phenomenon which isn't based on information presentation as framing effects are, but on information selection. Information selection is however not an unproblematic matter. Systematic selection of information may cause polarization of opinions to the extreme, which isn't particularly desirable for society and democracy.

Chapter 6
Polarized People

I think in our time, you know, so much of the information we get is pre-polarized

—George Saunders

6.1 Trouble Either way

Monica is 14 years of age and a zealous user of social media, not only Facebook, Instagram, and Twitter but also one of the recent additions to the pool of virtual interpersonal devices, *Formspring: Share your perspective on anything* (Budtz Pedersen et al. 2012). An anonymous derisive comment recently surfaced on Formspring aimed at a classmate who Monica, in passing, doesn't particularly care for. Now the classmate erroneously believes that Monica is responsible for the scornful and slanderous message. The classmate responds with "Thanks a bunch Monica, I'll see you on Monday" for everybody on the wall to see. It doesn't take long before comments of sympathy for the classmate begin to appear along with messages about how terrible and mean a person Monica really is. A courageous few try to argue differently, or suggest that perhaps Monica isn't the evil-doer. Soon enough these scarce voices fall silent and the remaining incoming commentaries almost exclusively come from friends and allies of the classmate. The more the messages bounce back and forth and participants deliberate over the matter, the meaner Monica apparently becomes in the eyes of the group. *People polarize.* It gets to the point where Monica decides to both delete her *Formspring* profile and not go to school on Monday fearing further reprisals.

But she hasn't done anything! That doesn't matter anymore, the damage is already done with no winning strategy left for Monica: If she shows up for school on Monday she has to protest her innocence against a narrative already established and grown sufficiently robust among schoolmates, friends and foes; if she stays home she is guilty by the associative action of not showing up. Either way, Monica is in trouble.

The polarization and deliberative dynamics in teenage online realms apparently extends all the way to current partisan polarization in, say, American politics, as recent studies show.[1] The partisan polarization of values and basic beliefs among American voters is today allegedly more pronounced than ever documented before;

---

[1] Pew Review Research Center (2012). "Partisan Polarization Surges in Bush, Obama Years." *People Press*, June 4.

V. F. Hendricks, P. G. Hansen, *Infostorms,* DOI 10.1007/978-3-319-03832-2_6,
© Springer International Publishing Switzerland 2014

particularly when it comes to the value gap between Democrats and Republicans. This gap now supersedes all other differences of gender, age, race or social class between the two parties. Both parties have in recent years decreased in size, but ostensibly become stronger in opinion or grown ideologically more homogenous. A growing number of Democrats characterize themselves as liberals while self-portrayed conservative Republicans continue to outnumber moderates by double up. The numbers of liberal and moderate Democrats even out. As to the quality of the politics, the two parties score about the same with respect to political betrothal while Republicans swerve by their ever-growing minimalist view on the role of government and their lack of support for the environmental agenda. Democrats are routinely secular and more socially liberal.

Where does this increase in party polarization in US politics come from? Recent studies in political science isolate a cadre of people as primary vehicles of polarization: *Party activists* (Layman et al. 2006). At least two factors should be taken into account when considering the polarizing influence of party activists. One relates to the fact that American party nominees are selected through party primaries and caucuses rather than picked by some board or group of party luminaries like in many other societies enjoying democracy. Thus, potential elective candidates need support from party activists who naturally in these contests are present in large numbers. The disproportionate number of party activists may thus help secure the party nomination for a potential candidate.

Party activists are disproportionately represented, not only quantitatively but also qualitatively insofar as their views tend to be more extreme than the average voter or party mass identifier. Purists and party activists are more radical in their views and less willing to compromise these views or back down from issues close to heart. Ideological incentives have here replaced political professionals and pragmatists. Thus activists tend to exercise decisive influence in the partisan change process. Activists shape ideologically rather extreme positions on new and challenging political issues. In fact, party activists among party activists have even grown more polarized along lines of firm ideology and stout political awareness as of late (Layman et al. 2005). *Polarized people polarize*—just think of the ideological standoff pertaining to Obamacare, the government shutdown, drinking tea and raising the debt ceiling.

6.2 Deliberating to the Extreme

An interesting statistical regularity has been documented pertaining to group deliberation. This phenomenon has been called *group* or *attitude polarization*, or just *polarization* for short. Polarization has been intensively studied by Harvard Law Professor and Administrator of the White House Office of Information and Regulatory Affairs (2009–2012), Cass.

> The basic idea is that deliberation tends to move groups, and the individuals who compose them, toward a more extreme point in the direction indicated by their own pre-deliberation judgments (Sunstein 2014).

Fig. 6.1 Polarization and
information selection

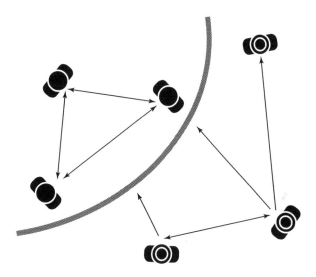

The mere discussion of, or deliberation over, a certain matter or opinion in a group
may entail that the position of the entire group *shifts* to a more radicalized version
of the view the group on average had prior to deliberation. It may also entail that
the point of view of each group member may shift to a more extreme version of the
viewpoint they each entertained before deliberating. The latter is often the hope of
party activists, although the shift of the entire group towards the more extreme is
often good enough for practical purposes of exercising influence, dictating the party
view or agenda on some issue or mobilizing the rank-and-file members of the party
to some desired end.

Polarization explains why it might not always be an advantage to be in the company
of like-minded people, or people sharing the same view, no matter how comfortable it
may seem. If we're already in agreement about something, we only grow to agree even
more by discussing the matter—and if we disagree, well, we'll get to that in a minute.

The danger of deliberation creeps in when you get to agree with other group peers
to an extent where it becomes extremism. This possibility begs material questions
about deliberation's role in the public space of heterogeneous democracies like most
Western ones. When like-minded peers participate in a sort of 'polarization game',
where they meet regularly, generally have similar preliminary conceptions, confirm
their viewpoints and refine their arguments to some end, and moreover aren't subjected too much to declarations of competing views or arguments from the outside,
staggered extreme viewpoints and groups become ever more likely (Cooper et al.
2004; Sunstein 2009).

Polarization, in contrast to pluralistic ignorance, is not the result of too little
information; neither is it the result of too much, as in case of informational cascades.
Nor is information presentation the culprit like in framing effects. The polarization
game indicates that excessive *information selection* i the problem by heavy-handed
filtering of the voices one is willing to listen to, the sources one is willing to read
and the people one is willing to talk to (Fig. 6.1).

If deliberation can push groups to more intransigent views than each individual originally had, is there any good reason to insist that deliberation should be part of bringing about improvement of democratic processes or clarification of issues in democracy? That individuals or groups may assume extreme convictions is hardly news, but if this insight is paired with the ideal of the deliberating democracy, a paradoxical situation surfaces: Deliberation is on one hand good since it's part of making the democratic form of government more robust. During the deliberation process it's possible to take disagreements, differences and opposing views into account, which is precisely the characteristic of an amalgamated and heterogeneous democracy with many diverse agents, interest groups and beliefs. Deliberation may on the other hand also be dangerous on its own as it may lead to monomania under certain circumstances. If recent history has taught us anything it is that democracy is vulnerable to extreme partisanship and especially extreme movements, which ultimately may give way to social instability, fragmentation and perhaps even downright violence, terrorism and war.

Finally, add to this that polarization may be both facilitated and amplified by modern information technology and we may be heading for yet another infostorm now based on information selection and more social proof if individuals at the outset are in doubt about which view to adopt or opinion to entertain.

6.3 Gnomes and People Like Us

There are millions of groups on social media with users converging on all kinds of common views or interests: "Physics Doesn't Exist, It's All Gnomes" had 23,347 members in the spring of 2013; "I wish life came with a remote to ◄◄ rewind ► play ‖ pause ►► fast forward" had 1.1 million members while "2013 largest group" as of February 2013 had 10 members on Facebook.

Just because people have common interests in gnomes or politics doesn't necessarily mean that people polarize accordingly, but of course search features of social networks may potentially stimulate polarization. Consider a social search-engine, which goes through the enormous amounts of data a social network has about its users.[2] What the search-engine does is to make it significantly easier to obtain information and the information received in response to queries is based on your network of friends and connections and the information they share. Which restaurants do your friends like in Greenwich Village or San Francisco?[3] The social search machine will reply with a list complete with links to whom of your friends have either visited

[2] Miner, Z. (2013). "Facebook launches Graph Search to all English speaking users, acknowledges privacy Concerns", *TechHive*, August 7, 2013: http://www.techhive.com/article/2046139/facebook-launches-graph-search-to-all-englishspeaking-users-acknowledges-privacy-concerns.html, accessed August 13, 2013.

[3] McGee, M. (2013), "Facebook Graph Search Then and Now: What's Changed", Search Engine Land, July 8, 2013: http://searchengineland.com/facebooks-graph-search-then-now-whats-changed-166052, accessed August 12, 2013.

the restaurants in question or mentioned them on the network. One may search for specific topics, which users are talking about for example music, thrillers, or games; you can search for people with the same interests as you, whether kite-surfing or work ambition. Now, the real force of the search-engine appears once search criteria are combined. A search string like "Music, which people who like Barack Obama, listen to"[4] will return a result tailored to unanimous people. The filtering of information may have begun—now potentially across unrelated topics. Again, excessive information selection is in essence what polarization is about. There is nothing particularly threatening or disconcerting about search strings like "Music, which people who like Barack Obama, listen to", but other search strings are more perplexing.

Experiments have been run on search strings like "People in a relationship who like adultery"; "People who like PETA and like Chinchilla fur coats"; "People who work as prostitutes" etc. All returned positive information about users and their network of friends.[5] This may of course be disturbing information for partners, co-members of The Foundation for Animal Protection (PETA) and an employer checking the profiles of job candidates. On a bad day, when the application is paired up with crowd-sourced recommendations or disapprovals from friends of friends of friends, the social search facility may be turned into a platform for the many like-minds to inadvertently rehearse points of view to the extreme, possibly facilitating everything from rumors to witch hunts of the few or other-minded groups: All of this, just because we initially searched for people like us.

6.4   Polarization Structure

Even though group polarization is one of the most robust patterns existing among deliberating assemblies, a particular logical structure and adherent dynamics must be in place before the polarization phenomenon justly may be said to have occurred (Hansen et al. 2013). Structurally, group polarization may occur in situations in which there are:

1. A set of agents.
2. An issue on which agents' degree of agreement can vary on a scale with neutral midpoint and two extreme poles.
3. A division of agents into sub-groups, which are homogeneous with respect to their degree of agreement relative to the midpoint.
4. A group deliberation process, in which agents are free to discuss their opinions and arguments.

---

[4] Bea, F. (2013). "Just a few examples of How Facebook Graph Search Will Embarrass you", *Digital Trends*: http://www.digitaltrends.com/social-media/embarassing-facebook-graph-search-results/?goback=.gmp_2138864.gde_2138864_member_209732931, accessed January 30, 2013.

[5] Bea, F. (2013). ibid.

Given such a situation, a sub-group is said to *polarize* or *shift* in the case that the product of the group discussion has shifted further towards the pole initially favored. The shift is measured by comparing the average of individual pre-discussion expressions of agreement with post-discussion expression. The latter may be attained by asking for post-discussion expressions from individual agents and finding the mean, by requesting the group to reach consensus, or by requiring that the group determines this value by majority vote.

Based on homogeneous group experiments much akin to the above in setup, several studies have documented group polarization. In Myers (1982) an overview of some of these studies is provided. Two examples include racial attitudes among high-school seniors and responses to fictive international military crises involving the USA among US army officers, ROTC[6] cadets and university students. In the former, students were divided into high-, medium- and low-prejudice groups, and following discussion it was seen that the high and low groups had polarized. The high group had moved from ~ 1.7 to ~ 3 on a scale from -4 to 4, with zero being neutral, -4 being low prejudice and 4 being high prejudice. The low group moved from ~ 2.8 to ~ 3.5. In the latter, groups consisting of respectively US army officers, ROTC cadets and university students were asked to choose between 10 responses ranging from bilateral negotiations to nuclear force. Here, students initially favored the softer responses, whereas officers recommended the more militant solutions. After discussion, these two groups polarized, whereas the ROTC cadets were more neutral in both pre- and post-discussion scores.

6.5   I Want to Be Just Like You All

To recap what a 'more extreme position' is should be determined with reference to the preceding beliefs, and may only be assessed with respect to the group's touchstone opinion prior to deliberation. Deliberation is a contributory cause of convergence toward an extreme viewpoint relative to the viewpoint prior to the deliberation. This may imply that if a group of anti-royalists with convictions of various strengths meet, they become even more anti-royalist collectively once they have discussed the matter in plenum. If we agree already on something, we will only agree more once we have talked it over.

At least two explanations have been put forward as to why group polarization occurs (Sunstein 2009). One concerns the desire for *social comparison.* Members want to be perceived positively by other members of a given group and would also like to view themselves in a positive light, for that matter. When we become aware of what others think or believe, we may be tempted to adjust our stance in favor of the currently dominating position.

---

[6] *U.S. Reserve Officers' Training Corps—a college-based training program*: http://www.goarmy. com/rotc.html, accessed March 10, 2013.

Humans may therefore end up assuming a position which is somewhat socially contorted in a given context. This was the case in the choice between risk-reducing and risk-increasing alternatives in the previous chapter. If you, for example, have a desire to be perceived as someone who only takes moderate chances, your attitude is partially determined by this desire. On the other hand, you don't necessarily know what sort of queer fish a moderate risk-seeker is until it has been uncovered what position others assume when it comes to taking chances. Individuals therefore reshuffle their viewpoints and judgements, partly to uphold their image in front of others, partly to uphold their own self-image. If you want to appear as a persevering worker in the workplace, both to your colleagues and to yourself, your understanding of perseverance is partly dictated by others' understanding hereof. If you become too persevering, you might be frowned upon since the group then views you as overambitious, and if you aren't persevering enough, you'll be frowned upon because you appear lazy. Both clash with the social comparison in a group setting.

Another important documented explanation of the polarization phenomenon may be found in the *convincing* or *authoritative arguments*, which a certain grouping endorses. If one, for instance, like Occupy Wall Street, is of the opinion that the US banking and financial system is far more responsible for the financial crisis than the general public and the administration, ones position will be partially influenced by the arguments presented and viewed by the Occupy Wall Street movement as the most convincing ones. The choice of arguments subsequently moves towards what the group collectively perceives as the most convincing. After all, when the individual members of the group are predisposed in a certain attitudinal direction, there will turn out to be an overly large number of arguments that veer in the same direction. In turn, the result of further deliberations would be shifting the members even further away, but however still based on their original position.[7]

Meanwhile there mustn't be too many arguments in play, and if there are, many will be weeded out during the deliberation process—more information selection in other words. Group members may have thought of quite a cluster, but not all arguments justifying their original attitude. During conference the arguments of a large group of people will be put forward and heard, but the final assemblage of arguments will be wrung in one direction or another, depending on the composition of the group. Such a filtering process will in the end lead to the extraction of essential arguments.

Polarization may however also lead to another outcome. Individuals may not be disposed to support extreme viewpoints, but would rather seek a middle position in the desire for social comparison. Even though you might actually have a fanatical viewpoint, you word it carefully so as not to appear extreme. When others then express support of your 2 cents' worth, the charge is thus removed, and you can say what you really believe, without beating around the bush. Polarization thus balances between being a socially regulating authority and a social mechanism leading in the worst case to partisanship.

---

[7] Polarization, social comparison issues and sources of authoritative arguments have also been shown to be prevalent phenomena on company boards, executive committees and other corporate bodies (Zuh 2009).

6.6   Group Polarization and Individual Marginalization

The polarization tendency increases both when group members can identify with a particular cause or quote and especially when the group as a whole can identify itself as a contrasting group to one or several other groups (Mackie and Cooper 1984). It follows almost by definition that marginalized groups are self-contrasting in precisely this way. Polarization in marginalized groups may help explain what lies behind hate mails and cyber-bullying, hate groups and hate-crimes (against homosexuals or immigrants). Members resort to physical violence against others to manifest their cause, and also to emphasize to themselves and to each other how socially comparable they are internally in the group. Gang wars, ethnic tensions, even wars and terrorist acts may be seen as examples of polarization of marginalized groups.

Polarization of groups is not the same as marginalization of individuals. One should think that social media—alas, even the very term "social media" suggests it—facilitate contacts and establish relations between people. One can unite with friends of old, ex-girlfriends and boyfriends, old classmates, ex-colleagues and distant relatives all of whom are but a click away. Re-uniting with people of the past is one usage, finding people of the present with similar political convictions, cultural interests or religious beliefs, is yet another usage. It has never been easier to find kindred spirits of this sort. It's simply a matter of a post on the wall and from here on other users may approve, countenance, "like", "smiley" or make other upvote gestures. The ones who disapprove refrain from answering and the filtering process has begun again and will continue for as long as immediate interest can be kept up or some breaking news appears which rouses renewed interest, sympathy, reflection or otherwise indignation, hostility or imprudence.

Does one become more social, develop more refined social skills or acquire a greater cross-cultural understanding when using social media? It would be conducive to humanity if this were true since we have to live with each other across borders, cultures and classes in a global world. Unfortunately it seems that our luck is not quite that good. Human commitment and tone of voice on the web and social media, as central vehicles of social comparison, arguments, competence and cross-cultural understanding, is virtual and by virtue not for real. New studies in social psychology and network information theory suggest that although we are more connected than ever before, due in large part to social media, we have never been lonelier and more narcissistic.

Yvette Vickers, a former B-movie actress, would most likely have turned 83 in 2012 but nobody knows exactly how old she was when she died. The Los Angeles Times reported that a neighbor found her dead in her home after a year, mummified in front of the computer, which was still on. Once the news broke—"Mummified Body of Former Playboy Playmate Yvette Vickers Found in Her Benedict Canyon Home"—was the headline in the *Los Angeles Times*,[8] the story instantly went viral.

---

[8] Blankenstein, A. (2012). "Mummified Body of Former Playboy Playmate Yvette Vickers Found in Her Benedict Canyon Home", Los Angeles Times, May 2, 2012: http://latimesblogs. latimes.com/lanow/2011/05/early-playboy-playmate-and-b-movie-acress-yvette-vickers-found-de ad-in-benedict-canyon.html, accessed August 16, 2013.

Within two weeks, Vickers' lonely death was the subject of 16,057 Facebook posts and 881 tweets. She had plenty of followers on social media at large as she was a horror-movie icon, and she had a sizable web of connections; this web was also apparently quite cursory, and so nobody online was aware that she had been dead for about a year.

A cautious conclusion, according to new social network analyses, seems to be that people who are already lonely spend more time on social media and become even lonelier. Direct human contact is replaced by impersonal and non-committal clicks and "likes", none of which makes a real difference or stimulate social skills, human interaction and understanding. As a matter of fact, one may increase social capital online with a lot of "likes", but it's a quantitative measure saying very little about the quality of the compiled "likes". What is known as "broadcasting" and "passive consumption" is outwardly correlated with feelings of disconnectedness. On the other hand, personal messages, called "composed communication", as opposed to "one-click communication" are more gratifying to receive. A recently conducted social experiment shows that people who received composed communication became less lonely, while people who received one-click communication experienced no difference in their loneliness.[9]

6.7 Dissolving Divarication

Polarization is, mind you, not necessarily a consequence of people gathering around the same cause, case or having a mutual interest in anything from microwave ovens to the current climate crisis. The phenomenon, especially in view of the question of democracy, is to a large extent conditioned by whether people perceive themselves as part of the same social grouping or rank as other members. A feeling of marginalized common identity and solidarity may on one hand make the shift more radical, but if the marginalized common identity and solidarity on the other hand is absent, it may either reduce the shift or completely dissolve it.

Deliberating groups additionally have a tendency to depolarize when they are built upon sub-groups which are equally strong in (oppositely)-directed beliefs, not least if the members exhibit some measure of flexibility. Furthermore, it's a statistical fact that some groups don't polarize, but end up with a common stance in the middle of the golden mean, in spite of intense internal discussion and debate. If defenders of the original stance are impossible to persuade one way or another, polarization has a hard time. External circumstances may counteract group polarization. Members of a given group having very clear and well-defined viewpoints about everything ranging from freedom of speech over state involvement, xenophobia to secularism may be disposed to polarize, but never do. To maintain a particular political agenda

---

[9] Marche, S. (2012)."Is Facebook Making us Lonely", *The Atlantic*, May, 2012: http://www. theatlantic.com/n. gazine/archive/2012/05/is-facebook-making-us-lonely/308930/, accessed August 16, 2013.

or credibility, the members of the group can be relatively moderate in their statements in the public sphere as well as in private. This may entail that groups who have begun to polarize toward the extreme can end up in the middle, because the position in the middle is a better measure to promote or conjure up political, social, economic or cultural legitimacy. Depolarization happens too, and deliberation without shifts may occur as well.

6.8 The Deliberative Democracy

Discussion and exchange of opinions are central elements of the *deliberative democracy*. Imprints of prompt public opinion are not the hallmark of smooth-running democracies (Sunstein 2009). Deliberation must alternatively be combined with plausible arguments and responsiveness so that civil alacrity in turn goes hand in hand with a process in which people swap information, opinions and ideas—even disagree. It's allegedly also why one many a time and oft hears opinion-formers, decision-makers and politicians say "Well, it's good we have started the debate on how to . . . ", " I wrote the opinion piece in order to kick off the discussion of . . . ", and so forth.

Given the polarization mechanism and conditions, deliberation is, however, not necessarily something to be glorified as an enlightenment boon or pursued as an information value in and by itself. Deliberation is not by itself a pass way to reason and truth. Information exchange can foster tilts which cannot be justified with reference to people being allowed to voice their attitudes, arguments or opinions, and definitely not if it's taking place in a controlled or downright isolated environment (Stasavage 2007).

A democracy is composed of the masses, and it's important to consider what the masses can strive to attain when it comes to reason and truth. In contrast to Plato's doubts about democracy, because what is true cannot be decided by majority vote, a new and more nuanced claim is that if one takes the average stance a given group endorses, it turns out to be surprisingly close to something truthful—the wisdom of crowds. Actually the *average* stance is much closer to something correct than the *majority's* stance.

The latter claim is often explained with reference to what in political and social science is known as *Condorcet's jury theorem* (List and Goodin 2001). This theorem rests on a series of assumptions. Firstly assume that a population must answer a question, which has two possible answers: One answer is true, and the other is false. Secondly assume that the likelihood that each respondent's answer will be correct is (just marginally) above 50 %. Condorcet's theorem now states that the likelihood that the majority of those polled will give a correct response increases steadily towards 100 % in line with the number of respondents increasing. Under the condition that a majority rule is applied, and each of the respondent's have more than a 50 % chance of answering correctly, the theorem states that individuals perform worse than groups when it comes to reaching the correct result—and the larger the group the better.

On August 8, 2013 at 1:16 p.m. there were 4,302,587 articles on the English version of Wikipedia as well as 19,463,598 users harvesting information about everything from garden gnomes to the Hubble Telescope, according to Wikipedia statistics.[10] Wikipedia rests on the idea that the more people contributing to the work and the more people contentiously correcting the information entered, the closer the information on Wikipedia comes to something genuinely correct. Wikipedia may therefore from the current perspective be seen as the incarnation of Condorcet's jury theorem for cyberspace encyclopaedias.[11]

The claim of the theorem is context-independent so it applies equally well to the union of librarians as it does to multinational stock exchange boards. It's also significant in parliament: If there is more than a 50 % probability that each representative of democracy has the correct attitude, the likelihood that the majority has the correct attitude in the passing of a resolution, the drafting of political declarations etc., is very high.

Condorcet's theorem is often recognized as a technical result which supports the idea of democracy as the best form of government. Meanwhile there is a flipside, if one simply reverses one of the assumptions: Assume that each of the respondents has more than a 50 % probability of answering incorrectly instead of correctly, while the assumption of the majority rule is left unaltered. In that case the probability that the majority answers correctly moves toward 0 % as the number of respondents increase. That's not quite so good news.

Even if you imagine that the average stance of a large group is correct, deliberation may still prove to be rather interrupting and lead to graver errors and decisions—those are presumably the terms of the polarization phenomenon. Should this come to mean that there is no room in democracy for deliberation and that everyone, from the family in Anchorage, Nebraska to the social club in London to the board of the business conglomerate operating out of Dubai, are better served with mere choice actions without a preceding exchange of views? Hardly, but it does still mean that the idea of deliberation itself should be further itemized, that it's not simply a boon on its own, and that there are requirements to be met by both the deliberation process as such and those participating in it. More precisely it follows according to Sunstein that:

> A system of deliberation is likely to work well if it includes diverse people—that is, if it has a degree of diversity in terms of approaches, information, and positions. Cognitive diversity is crucial to the success of deliberative democracy and it's analogous in the private sector. (Sunstein 2009, pp. 142–143).

New computer simulations of the polarization phenomenon meanwhile suggest that once polarization occurs, it truly requires some unflinching opponents to put a stop to it again (Olsson 2011): Actually so unflinching that the opponents are almost immune to shifts of viewpoints—but that is on the other hand also somewhat extreme!

---

[10] http://en.wikipedia.org/wiki/Wikipedia:Statistics, accessed August 8, 2013.

[11] Wikipedia is also supplemented by a number of moderators and editors installed to staunch vandalism and secure merit of the entries.

6.9   Echo-Chambers and Stomping Grounds

Groups like

- *After Monday & Tuesday even the Calendar says W T F . . .*
- *"Dammit I'm mad" is the same spelt backwards! Mind blowing isn't it,* and
- *If 1,000,000 people join this group, nothing will happen*

can hardly be suspected of giving rise to malicious social, political or religious fragmentation, but there are other groups on the many social media platforms and dedicated blog sites which very well may.[12] What these installations have in common is that they may serve as *echo chambers* at worst, where one over and over lends ear to repetitions of one's own conviction from fellow partisans. The lack of new, extraneous and competing expressions of opinion can motivate fragmentation in society, which is neither innocent let alone beneficial from a social, political or religious point of view. In line with the ever growing information specialization and—screening on the web and in the media, one may with more or less cunning and finesse construct profoundly individualized communication packages, which filter annoying voices and incompatible noisy information out, that one doesn't care to listen to. Group polarization can henceforth be part of explaining why fragmented communication markets may cause societal problems—see the following chapter on bubbles.

For deliberative democracy there are desired advantages of small closed *stomping grounds* of fellow partisans. In composite and dissimilar societies, as for instance the Western democracies, there will be members of various demographic groups who have a hard time being heard in large assemblies. The benefit of corner confabulation on the web and elsewhere is, therefore, that it may promote the development of positions and premises and refine viewpoints or arguments, which would otherwise have been invisible or stifled in the public debate, since they are either too much, too strange or too suspicious.

In larger deliberating assemblies it's a fact that members with a high rank, like presidents, chairmen, pioneering initiators, instigators, founders and the like, typically are those who kick-off debate and lead the pending discussion, and whose ideas have most clout. Members of lower rank and file don't have the same confidence in their own abilities and maybe fear what the expression of their candid opinion might bring about in terms of social indignation, reprisals or stigmatization. Studies of these regrettable washouts speak volumes: Women's ideas often have less sway or are blatantly suppressed in mixed gender groups, and cultural minorities have less to say on a matter and less influence on decisions made in mixed culture groups. It could end up in self-reinforcing censure, which goes hand in hand with pluralistic ignorance and accelerates to an infostorm by the use of information technology.

---

[12] If for no other reason than because it is easy to find like-minded people using your virtual bullhorn to world and publics.

6.10 Deaf, Blind and Mute

The relationship between deliberation and democracy is a delicate matter, when group polarization is acknowledged. Deliberation should ideally take place within the framework of a large, composite view exchanging public sphere, in order to escape situations where fellow partisans isolate themselves from seesaw stances and differential perspectives.

Proponents of the deliberative democracy ideal often refer to prerequisites like political equality and humans not acting strategically or opportunistically but rather in accordance with fundamental beliefs and perfect information, as well as the joint goal of reaching mutual understanding and preferably agreement. All these are commendable qualities and preconditions, and especially political equality amongst citizens is indeed a fix point. But in everyday life we are often strategically conniving, and that also applies to affairs or decision situations, where access is granted to all available information—the complete public space as an open information structure as described in Chap. 3. One could perhaps reduce or completely remove polarization, if one as a prerequisite for good and healthy deliberation had an indispensable requirement of complete information, since the cluster of arguments and good reasons to hold on to a particular stance then wouldn't be limited by possible information selection. But even if you imagine a ban on information selection, which all parties and groups involved adhered to, such a provision isn't sufficient to guarantee that deliberation is actually truth-tracking. To deliberate on a perfectly informed basis does not alone guarantee that you sooner or later converge to something correct.

The artifice of a smooth-running democracy consists in creating institutions which ensure that deliberation is on the narrow track of truth—the National Auditors, the ombudsman institution, miscellaneous commissions etc. One should simultaneously incite that polarization, if it should after all occur, is the result of education, enlightenment, and knowledge rather than arbitrary group dynamics and random idiosyncratic decision-making.

With the plethora of information and its appertaining noise one can turn deaf; with deliberation lacking diverse information one can become blind; with polarized extremism one can grow mute. Without certain well-chosen, truth-tracking institutions and methods of inquiry, democracy runs the risk of turning deaf, blind and mute worst case.

Chapter 7
Bubbles

If something is going on, Twitter is the place to go to get the fastest information (...) It's gonna get there first and it might not be the full story. That is where you have to wait for other established news sources to comment and do legwork on your own.

—Jeffrey Kleintop, LPL Financial

7.1 Financial Bubbles

The term "bubble" has traditionally been associated with a particular situation occurring on financial markets:

A bubble is considered to have developed when assets trade at prices that are far in excess of an estimate of the fundamental value of the asset, as determined from discounted expected future cash flows using current interest rates and typical long-run risk premiums associated with asset class. Speculators, in such circumstances, are more interested in profiting from trading the asset than in its use or earnings capacity or true value (Vogel 2010, p. 16).

Textbook examples of bubbles include the Dutch tulip bulbs frenzy in the 1600s, the South Sea and Mississippi excesses about a century later, the US stock market as of 1929, the Japanese real-estate and equity markets of the 1980s, the dot.com period and Internet stock boom of the 1990s, and of course the balloons, frenzies and speculative mania in the world economy leading to the global financial crisis of 2008 of which we are still in the midst of the aftermath.

In wake of the current crisis there have been many suggestions as to why financial bubbles occur, most of them composites in terms of explanatory factors involving different mixing ratios of bubble-hospitable market configurations and social psychological features of human nature and informational phenomena like the ones discussed here in *Infostorms* (Hendricks and Lundorff-Rasmussen 2012).

One seemingly paradoxical hypothesis suggests that too much liquidity is actually poisonous rather than beneficial for a financial market (Buchanan 2008). Monetary liquidity in excess stimulated by easy access to credit, large disposable incomes and lax lending standards combined with expansionary monetary policies of lowering interests by banks and advantageous tax breaks and bars by the state, flush the market with capital. This extra liquidity leaves financial markets vulnerable to volatile asset price inflation, the cause of which is to be found in short-term and possibly leveraged speculation by investors.

V. F. Hendricks, P. G. Hansen, *Infostorms,* DOI 10.1007/978-3-319-03832-2_7,
© Springer International Publishing Switzerland 2014

The situation becomes such that too much money chases too few assets, good as well as bad, both of which in return are elevated well beyond their fundamental value to a level of general unsustainability. Pair up too much liquidity with robustly demonstrated socio-psychological features of human nature like boom-thinking, group-thinking, herding, informational cascades and other aggregated phenomena of social proof, it only becomes a matter of time before the bubbles start to burst (Lee 1998)—at least in finance.

However, behind every financial bubble, crash and subsequent crisis "lurks a political bubble—policy biases that foster market behaviors leading to financial instability"—to cite McCarty, Poole and Rosenthal (2013) with reference to the 2008 financial crunch. Thus there are political bubbles too . . . and other sorts as well.

7.2 Bubble Sorts

There are stock, real-estate and other bubbles associated with financial markets but also filter bubbles, opinion bubbles, political bubbles, science bubbles, social bubbles, status bubbles, fashion bubbles, art bubbles . . . all pushing collectives of agents in the same (sometimes unfortunate) direction; not only buying the same stock or real-estate but also thinking the same thing, holding the same opinions, appreciating the same art, "liking" the same posts on social media, upvoting the same reviews on online rating systems, purchasing the same brand names, subscribing to the same research program in science etc.

Internet activist Eli Pariser coined the term "filter bubble" (Pariser 2011) to refer to selective information acquisition by website algorithms (in search-engines, news feeds, flash messages, tweets, RSS) personalizing search results for users based on past search history, click behavior and location, and accordingly filtering away information in conflict with user interest, viewpoint or opinion: An automated but personalized information selection process in line with the polarization mechanics described in the previous chapter that isolate users in their cultural, political, ideological or religious bubbles. Filter bubbles may stimulate individual narrow-mindedness but are also potentially harmful to the general society, undermining informed civic or public deliberation, debate and discourse and making citizens ever more susceptible to propaganda and manipulation:

> A world constructed from the familiar is a world in which there's nothing to learn . . . (since there is) invisible autopropaganda, indoctrinating us with our own ideas (Pariser 2011, *The Economist*, June 30).

Harvesting or filtering information in a particular way is part of aggregating opinion. One may invest an opinion on the free market place of ideas and a certain idea or stance, whether political, religious or otherwise, may at a certain point gain popularity or prominence and become an asset by virtue of the number of people apparently subscribing to it in terms of likes, upvotes, clicks or similar endorsements of minimum personal investment. Public opinion tends to shift depending on a variety of factors ranging from zeitgeist, new facts, what people think others now think and current interests, to premiums of social imprimatur. Opinion bubbles may suddenly go bust or gradually deflate accordingly.

Everyday personal opinions can serve as intellectual liquidity chasing assets of political or cultural ideas. But scientific inquiry may also be geared with too much intellectual liquidity in terms of explanatory expectations and available funding, paired up with boom-thinking in the scientific community. The short-term and possibly leveraged speculation by scientists may exactly occur in the way characterizing a ballooning market—science bubbles emerge (Budtz Pedersen and Hendricks 2013). The modern commercialization of science and research has even been compared to downright Ponzi-schemes, only surviving as long as you can steal from Peter to pay Paul scientifically, so to speak (Mirowski 2013).

Fashion in particular relies on getting everybody, or a select few, to trend the same way—that's the point of the entire enterprise besides the occasional claim to artistic diligence. The same goes for the status bubbles of status economics described in Chap. 2.

But even the art scene is tangibly ridden with bubbles: "The bubble that is Con Art blew up, like the sub-prime mortgage business, in the smoke-and-mirrors world of financial markets, where fortunes have been made on nothing" says Julian Spalding to *The Independent* (March 26, 2012); the famous British gallery owner was commenting on his recent book Con Art—Why you ought to sell your Damien Hirst's while you can (2012).

> The concept of bubbles appears in seemingly different spheres. Perhaps it is more than just terminological coincidence—across spheres bubbles share similar structure and dynamics—from science to society.

7.3 Science Bubbles

Overly optimistic investments in specific areas of science research, methodologies and technologies generate states comparable to the ones financial markets are in prior to crashing (Budtz Pedersen and Hendricks 2013).

The cause of the meltdown of the financial market is related to leveraged trading in financial instruments that bear no relation to the things they are supposed to be secured against (Gerrans 2009). Science, too, is a market in which the value of research is ultimately secured against objects in the world or facts about it. A paper that claims that smoking causes cancer or that terrorism is caused by poverty is valuable only if it turns out to be a good explanation of cancer or terrorism as the phenomena appear out there. As noted by Gerrans (2009) "that is why an original and true explanation is the gold standard of academic markets".

Consider the recent investments in neuroscience. No one with even a passing interest in scientific trends and science policy will have failed to notice that cognitive neuroscience may be the next big thing. This narrative has been around for at least a decade, but now it is getting serious—with, for example, the recent award by the European Commission of € 500 million (US$ 646 million) to the Human Brain

Project to build a new "infrastructure for future neuroscience" (Abbott 2013), and the 1-billion USD Brain Activity Map Project endorsed by President Obama in January 2013. The Brain Activity Map is said to be "the largest and most ambitious effort in fundamental biology since the Human Genome Project" (Wadman 2013, p. 19).[1]

As with a leveraged investment in mortgage bonds, most policy-makers have little or no competence in determining how these megaprojects will turn out. It is like an investor predicting the market. Whether or not the expectations will be realized, research funding is framed with expectations that neuroscience will translate into jobs and growth. Neurotechnology (brain-based devices, drugs and diagnostics) is projected to be a 145 billion USD industry by 2025 (Robinson 2010). Correspondingly, the science system has seen an unprecedented rise in fields that attach "neuro" to some human behavior or trait—such as neuroeconomics, neuromarketing, neuropsychiatry, neuroethics, neuro-criminology and so on—with the discounted expectation that the techniques of neuroscience will explain the relevant human behavior. In fact, the grand vision of neuroscience seems to have taken an unforeseen turn. The proposed research agenda has put the focus on the explanation of *all* human cognition and behavior. That's an expectantly compelling vision, so how do you get into the neuroscience game?

Every social coordination game consists of two sets of logically distinct rules: (1) constitutive rules making the game the game it is. The constitutive rules of chess, for instance, include the specifications of the allowed movements of the different chess pieces, the layout of the boards etc.: (2) regulatory rules pertaining to how well you play the game, for instance, the reward you are given for winning, or the strategies adopted for opening, attacking, or closing a game. The goal of chess is to win against your opponent in the legitimate way specified by the constitutive rules. However, if the constitutive and regulatory rules get out of synch, winning may become more important than playing. In this case, the regulatory rules may lead playing agents to set aside the constitutive rules. Instead, the agents will start speculating in eluding the rules (cheating, doping, etc.) or changing the game altogether. Then again, you don't really win according to what the game is: You change the rules, and that's a different game altogether.

Science may be compared to a game the objective of which is to find true, adequate or correct models of relevant aspects of the world using the methods of scientific inquiry as the constitutive framework. The regulatory rules are comprised of everything from publication strategies, incentive structures and directives for research organization, to management and funding. In science, one may play according to the regulatory rules while heading nowhere near a correct model. Boosting results and doping scientific findings beyond their explanatory value may indeed be an optimal

---

[1] As reported by *Nature* the idea for the Brain Activity Map was born by a group of neuroscientists in 2011. The contours of the project and the argument for investing in neuroscience were laid out in a white paper which stated that neuroscientists were "on the verge to illuminate . . . the impenetrable jungles of brain functions, by mapping and stimulating neural circuits with cellular and millisecond-level resolution". The paper, which eventually appeared in *Neuron* (A.P. Alivisatos et al. *Neuron* 74, 970–974; 2012), was handed over to the White House's Office of Science and Technology Policy (OSTP) and accepted for funding in 2013.

strategy for acquiring short-term rewards, such as funding or some other research benefits, but it does not do the goal of knowledge-acquisition any good. On the contrary, it undermines the scientific goal even if it optimizes certain other features of scientific research according to instilled regulatory principles. Pursuit of adequacy, truth or correctness according to the constitutive rules of science and optimization according to the regulatory rules of science management do not necessarily entail each other. They indeed define two different investment games, unfortunately sometimes conflated by speculators ranging from researchers themselves to university managers and funding agencies. Because scientists are constantly competing for resources at ever more diverse levels, they are encouraged to push their arguments to the limit, and sometimes off the map, and exaggerate the merits of scientific explanations. As Rip explains, "a strategic game is being played . . . in which being first is more important than going in the right direction" (Rip 2009, p. 669). That is a point of optimization rather than reliable truth-conducive scientific inquiry.

Now, to facilitate a bubble in finance, assets must be traded above their fundamental value leaving speculators to take a risk investing their means but hoping for later positive returns. The fundamental value of an asset is determined by the expected future pay-off, which again is based on current interest rates and long-term risk premiums. There must be a reward for taking a risk: That is, the minimum amount of money that an expected return on an asset has to exceed given the known return on a risk-free asset like, for instance, bonds.

The situation of a scientist in such a bubble game is not unlike the one of the investor. In reverse order, the risk-free asset corresponds to finding a true, adequate or correct scientific hypothesis, which is a risk-free asset as long as the constitutive rules of science are observed. The risky asset, on the other hand, corresponds to jumping the bandwagon of optimization in some research field, which has not yet cashed in expectations of explanation and scientific insight. As long as the risk premium in terms of recognition, reward, and workload (in this sense place-holders for current interest rates) outweighs the narrow pursuit of truth, adequacy, or correctness this provides a workable incentive: The individual scientist will run with optimization (given by the regulatory rules of science management) as long as the bubble doesn't burst before he or she retires. If the field of inquiry is geared with too much intellectual liquidity in terms of explanatory expectations and available funding, the short-term and possibly leveraged speculation by scientists may occur exactly in the way characterizing a bubble in the market.

One of the problems pertaining to financial bubbles is to fix exactly what is meant by fundamental value (Vogel 2010). Still, a bubble may burst once it is realized that the asset has oversold itself. In science it is the same. We may not exactly know the true or adequate model but scientific inquiry as such has proved successful in falsifying incorrect theories and avoiding malpractices. At the end of the day, a science bubble will be confronted by accumulated evidence and theory. Scientific knowledge does not answer well to investor mechanics and speculation; neither should scientists or their knowledge products:

> When scientists mobilize resources, as well as when they present their products to audiences,
> they have to *justify* their actions and their products (...) Their success does not depend on
> a market taking up their products, but on their justification being accepted. In a comparable
> way, the production of authoritative decisions in democracy cannot proceed in a purely
> technical way, but depends critically on justifications and their acceptance (Rip 1988, p. 63).

Scientific truth, adequacy or correctness is non-negotiable. No price-fixing mechanism is able to determine truth-values according to the dynamics of supply and
demand. Optimizing outputs and justifying beliefs simply belong to two different
functional regimes.

According to conventional thinking in philosophy of science, bubbles in science
may regularly occur but are fairly harmless. On most occasions speculation and
overselling in science will not be allowed to balloon into fully-fledged bubbles. This
is because, in general, stocks in science—research papers, grant applications and
academic positions—are believed to trade fairly close to their truth-value (Gerrans
2009). Scientific norms such as organized peer review and collegial assessment
ensure that scientists are regularly confronted with counter-hypotheses, competing
theories and criticism. Other scientists want to check whether the theory is justified, if
the prediction is verified, if the theorem holds and if the relevant object is adequately
described.

With the changing organization and administration of research in most Western
countries, financial incentives and reward structures are replacing traditional scientific norms (Ziman 2001; Nowotny et al. 2001; Mirowski 2013). These incentives
include measures to stimulate research performance based on an increased competition among institutions and individuals; a growing pressure to publish in high-impact
journals; increased use of citation data in allocation of posts and funding; a growing demand for commercialization and patenting; and an increased use of university
rankings and benchmarking (Gläser and Whitley 2007). With the pervasive role of
evaluation exercises and extrinsic incentives, the balance between internal (block-
based) and external (performance-based) funding has changed. The effects of this
shift in emphasis and composition of funding have been fundamental to the organization of research. Previous studies suggest that a number of unintended consequences
and crowding-out effects may occur:

Firstly, when reward is given to the number of publications, researchers start to
concentrate more on problems that may lead to publishable results than on scientific
approaches that break away from the mainstream. This creates a "culture of compliance" limiting the proliferation of unorthodox ideas, leads to conservatism in peer
review, and induces risk-aversion among scientists and editors (Laudel 2006).

Secondly, the use of bibliometric evaluation and reward structures have created
a publication culture in which scientists are encouraged to slice their findings up
as much as possible (four papers are better than two). This creates a publication
bias in favor of publishing clear-cut, small-scale experimental studies, and against
publishing null-effects, replications, or developing extensive theoretical frameworks.
With editors favoring the publication of positive results, researchers will file negative
(i.e., null) findings in the drawer (Button et al. 2013).

Thirdly, in trying to satisfy external funding agencies, studies suggest that researchers are increasingly framing their claims in ways that are opportunistic to policymakers and external evaluators. Researchers stage their research questions, methodologies, and even theoretical approaches, according to the criteria defined by the funding programs and research councils (Weingart 2005; Budtz Pedersen 2013).

These consequences stimulate a situation in which the scientific personnel are incentivized to leverage their academic products and hence try to optimize their investments while passing on the academic products to peers, funding agencies and the general public while taking a fee by being symbolically (or monetarily) rewarded for the number of publications, citations, and patents etc.

Much has been written about the current economic crisis. Subprime loans were granted to insolvent borrowers by irresponsible financial institutions. Shares and other financial products were over-packaged, over-rated and over-sold. Very few economists anticipated how expectations fueled by false promises would cause the financial world to shake on its foundations. With the increasing use of performance indicators and reward compliance, similarities are to be found between the over-blown ambitions in the financial sector and those in the scientific market. In the realm of modern science, promises and hype have become widespread.

This is not to say that the current state of neuroscience, or any other field, is to be considered as a science bubble. It is rather argued that the intensity of expectations in pair with the concentration of liquidity makes science, like any other investment market, prone to bubble characteristics. Science is a highly rationalized practice considered from the standpoint of its constitutive rules. However, with the regulatory principles that are currently installed in scientific institutions, science may begin to exhibit bubble-behavior identifiable from the same principles that are governing the financial markets.

Irrational group behavior fuels bubbles. Individual scientists may have doubts about the merits of bibliometric evaluation or excessive publishing practices. However, a strong public signal aggregated by the previous actions and endorsements of colleagues and institutions suggesting an aggressive publication strategy and abiding to the regulatory rules of evaluation and funding schemes may suppress the personal doubt of the individual scientist. But when personal information gets suppressed in favor of a public signal regulating individual behavior it may in turn initialize a lemming-effect, an informational cascade. Now, informational cascades have proven to be robust features in the generation of financial bubbles, where "individuals choose to ignore or downplay their private information and instead jump the bandwagon by mimicking the actions of individuals acting previously" (Vogel 2010, p. 85).

Publishing in the journals everybody else publishes in, publishing only on the same topics, applying for funding for the same type of research projects, while at the same time expecting everybody else to play along, create a self-enforcing optimization game. In this environment science bubbles may grow and start to cash in the expectations or eventually go bust depending on whether they continue to abide by the constitutive rules of science or just follow the regulatory rules for optimizing funding and reward. As long as you can feed the beast of expectation with new research publications, spurious findings and low-powered studies, the bubble will keep growing steadily until truth, adequacy or correctness will eventually collapse it—with an investor confidence crisis following. Independently of whether the many scientific expectations will be realized, they are already changing the research land-scape. Overly optimistic research programs and claims of future scientific impacts crowd out more modest and pluralist research strategies pursued by scientists in search of novel explanations and solid evidence-building. The difference in crash characteristics is that financial markets go bust with a bang while science bubbles fizzle out (Budtz Pedersen and Hendricks 2013).

7.4   Opinion Bubbles and Conviction Peaks

In the movie *Wall Street* from 1987, tycoon Gordon Gekko, aka Michael Douglas, uttered the immortal lines:

> The most *valuable* commodity I know of is information.

Indeed, on the morning of January 22, 2013 a story started to develop on Twitter to the effect that the CEO of Deutsche Bundesbank, Jens Weidmann, was unexpectedly about to resign. The DAX index on the Frankfurt Stock Exchange soon started to drop and the euro came under severe pressure.

The first documented tweet at 10.02 a.m. pertaining to the resignation may be traced back to an anonymous blog profile called Russian Market with approximately 40,000 followers. In 25 min the information had been exposed 256,634 times and already at 10.20 a.m. the euro had gone from 1,3340 to 1,3267 against USD, dropping 0.55 % in value. Decimal movements may seem insignificant but given the heavy gearing of the international currency markets, exorbitant amounts of money may be made on micro movements if you can control the fluctuations and have this information prior to all other investors.

In this short time span, the rumor was not only tweeted and re-tweeted by wild stock/currency market desperados and self-appointed experts but also by more estab-lished parties in the business like bank stock-traders and even some finance editors of established newspapers. When authoritative quarters start to flag an unsubstantiated rumor as significant information it all of a sudden exactly becomes more substanti-ated and robust as arguments from authority in polarization dynamics show. Thus, when a spokesman from the Deutsche Bundesbank issued an official denial of the rumor which hit Twitter at 10:20 AM via the *Dow Jones/Wall Street Journal* it was with the rather strong wording "Komplette Blödsinn" meaning "Utter Garbage", which was also the headline of the first mention of the incident by Bloomberg News at 10:26 a.m. At 10:27 a.m. the official denial of Jens Weidmann's resignation had been shared 344,863 times on Twitter and in the meantime the euro had re-stabilized to its value prior to the false hearsay.[2]

---

[2] "Sociale børsdesperadoer spreder panik", *Berlingske Business*, March 18, 2013.

The Weidmann rumor is not a singularity—social media have more than once been used as vehicles for spreading junk evidence exciting the markets in unfortunate ways. In late January 2013 shares of Silicon Valley-based Audience Inc. dropped 25 % in seconds after a false tweet concerning a fraud investigation against the company started to proliferate; Cambridge-based biotech company Sarepta Therapeutics recently saw its stock plunge some 9 % when wrongfully accused of swindling—the erroneous narrative again starting on social media; finally, on April 23, 2013 an Associated Press "hoax tweet" claiming "Breaking: Two Explosions in the White House and Barack Obama is Injured" crashed the US stock market in minutes and caused the CBOE Volatility Index, also known as "the fear index", to surge 10 %. By way of numbers, the S&P 500, the NASDAQ and crude oil all dropped 1 % and the broader market apparently lost almost USD 200 billion according to USA Today.[3] The panic-selling was short-lived and the markets soon recovered most of the ground lost, but there is certainly something to be said for the power of information and emergence of either opinion bubbles or just short-lived conviction peaks on social media and in the press broadly construed.

Every user of the web has a voice to a public. Groups of users; miscellaneous interest groups, investor groups, political parties and grassroots, religious organizations etc. have websites and discussion forums serving the double-purpose of informing and filtering information at the very same time. When an investor is considering new assets to place money on, assessing the fundamental value of the asset presents a challenge. One has to fix the risk premium while considering the expected interest rate of the investment. Such expectations are often based on the historical return of the asset combined with the general zeitgeist (concerning, say, green energy, climate awareness, regional stability) and the whole investment group's expectations and actual investment in the asset. Collective boom-thinking within the group may drive the expected return to unrealistic levels. If the return cannot cash in the expectations, the fundamental value of the asset has been overestimated and a bubble has occurred.

Besides boom-thinking, "group polarization is at work as well, leading people to greater and greater confidence in a relatively extreme belief" (Sunstein 2009, p. 103) pertaining to the expected returns of the asset combined with a group tendency to cling on to believing what they previously believed and hence want to believe. This is much easier than acquiring new beliefs, contracting old ones, and revising the remaining (Vogel 2010, p. 79).

A single person voicing some extreme view, or conveying some warped information, means nothing, but a single person with 40,000 followers makes for a loud bullhorn to a public. Publics overlap, web robots constantly scout for "loud" information which is of interest to some public, filter bubbles are sorting information on an individual basis. It doesn't matter whether it is information about finance, religion, politics, people, art, science, or fashion. Conditions may be perfect for an opinion

---

[3] "SEC, FBI probe fake tweet that rocked stocks", USA Today, accessed April 24, 2013, http://www.usatoday.com/story/news/nation/2013/04/23/hack-attack-on-associated-press-shows-vulnerable-media/2106985/.

epidemic to spread as an unreflective contagion where everybody thinks what everybody else thinks even if only a very few, or no one, thinks such and so. There is just too much opinion out there and it costs very little or nothing at all to voice it—and if you don't have a strong opinion about something, you can always just "like" or upvote somebody else's.

"Like" is the predominant gesture on many social media. Depending on cause and context the gesture may indicate sympathy, respect, encouragement, acknowledgement, recognition, and attention, all of which have a positive or at least neutral connotation. Sometimes it is immediately clear how a "like" is to be interpreted, at other times abundantly obscure.

The positive or neutral application of a "like" was an important premise in the argument originally provided for only being able to "like" or upvote as opposed to "dislike" or downvote among users. Whether this ambition may be cashed in will largely depend on the particular case in question and the framing for the submission of "likes" or upvotes. A violently misogynistic page where parties gather around their common interest in raping women and celebrating sexual assaults,[4] or an interest group united by their predilection for decapitations[5] have many "likes" or upvotes but obviously neither because of positive content nor tone.

A "like" or upvote may be a simple and efficient way to share content by creating a link on some social media between the "like"-user and the material in question as already noted earlier. Some social media also issue network "like" action graphs, displaying stories on the "like"-user's timeline also appearing on news feeds of friends which in turn may drive distribution even further across multiple publics.

But, "like"- or upvote—expressions are ambiguous; what is it that you really like?

- Is it that somebody has created a page with some content you believe should be a public focal point even if you do not sympathize with the cause or case?
- Is it because you agree with the point of view advocated or share the same interest?
- Is it because you find collective commiserating amusing in a troll sort of way?;
- Is it because you want to celebrate the supposed freedom attached to putting up the page in the first place on the free market of ideas and opinions?
- Or . . . ?

Thus "likes" or upvotes may mean many things to different parties, from positive to negative, from approval to disapproval, from sympathy to disgust and the frame, perspective or context only seldom reveal *why* individuals, as well as groups, have registered their "likes" or upvotes.

---

[4] The *Guardian*, Thursday, April 8, 2013: http://www.theguardian.com/commentisfree/2013/apr/18/ facebook-big-misogyny-problem, retrieved August 12, 2013 and *Facebook*, May 28, 2013; (https:// www.facebook.com/notes/facebook-safety/controversial-harmful-and-hateful-speech-on-facebook/ 574430655911054, retrieved August 12, 2013.

[5] *BBC News Technology*, May 1, 2013: http://www.bbc.co.uk/news/technology-22368287, accessed August 12, 2013.

A "like" or some other upvote gesture is a virtual utterance. Utterances are *speech acts*. One should accordingly distinguished between the *locution*—the act of performing an utterance; the *illocution*—the significance of the utterance as a social verbal act, wish, hope, threat, inspire, . . . ; and finally the *perlocution*—the effect of the utterance; to persuade, to inform, to threat, to inspire, to . . . (Austin 1975). Now if "likes" are ambiguous, the illocutionary and perlocutionary acts become ambiguous as well even if the illocution is presented as unambiguous by a "thumps-up".

Individual "likes" or upvotes may seem insignificant, cost-neutral and innocent, but the *aggregation* of "likes" can make for a very potent public signal that others may take into account when deciding what to believe or do, i.e. in terms of seeking social proof. Now, if the public signal on top of that is ambiguous between recognition and revulsion, "liking" or upvoting may become highly disconcerting gestures with a lot of signal noise potentially creating more chaos than clarity.

It is a bit like rushing to Grand Central trying to catch the last train to Hoboken from Manhattan and the public announcement gets garbled right after "The train to Hoboken . . . *!?#/&%@§!" At what time? From what platform? It is going to be hard to deliberate, decide and act on this public information alone. So you start looking around to see what others who you think are going to Hoboken are doing. First of all, they may be looking back at you since they are in doubt as well, and second, none of you know for sure who is going to Hoboken anyway so the social proof established from aggregated uncertainty is unreliable at best although you would all "like" to go to Hoboken.

7.5 Bubble Trouble

At 5:16 a.m. on November 7, 2012 Barack Obama wrote "Four more years" on his Twitter profile when it was clear that a second term in the White House was secured. Within 3 h the message was re-tweeted 507,745 times and favored 173,028 times, making it the most popular tweet ever, beating a previous high-score tweet by Justin Bieber. The attached picture of Barack and Michelle Obama embracing was shared in the thousands among the 34 million fans. According to Twitter, the 2012 US election tops the list of tweet-attention of American politics with 31 million tweets on Election Day. When the TV-networks announced the victory, Twitter went berserk with an average of some 327,452 election-related tweets a minute.[6]

President Obama did not announce his second victory via the national news networks first, but instead used the social media to immediately reach 34 million fans with a truthful message travelling at the speed of light. *First*, if not best, *then breaking news* belongs to the social media and social networks now. Truth and falsity travel at

---

[6] *The Telegraph,* November 7, 2012: http://www.telegraph.co.uk/news/worldnews/us-election/9660533/Barack-Obamas-four-more-years-tweet-most-popular-ever.html. Retrieved August 12, 2013.

the same speed so there is still a paramount role to be played by the more traditional press even if they stand to lose the race for breaking.

Rephrasing Gordon Gekko:

The most *valuable* commodity I know of is *knowledge*,

but knowledge is significantly harder to obtain than information, and doesn't derail you once you have it as information very well may. Knowledge is anchored in truth; information, belief, opinion are not necessarily so and this matters on a market of convictions.

Let's try to make the analogy between opinions and finance bubbles a bit more precise. Now, in classical economic theory a perfectly *competitive market* requires (1) that products traded are homogenous in the sense that buyers and sellers don't have a preference for one product rather than another, and (2) no participants are so influential, or have such extensive market power, that they alone may set the price of the homogenous products traded. In the pure competition model buyers have varying degrees of willingness to pay for the product depending on price, and sellers have similarly varying degrees of willingness to sell depending accordingly. The market price for the product is determined by assuming that the buyers with the highest willingness to pay engage transaction to the lowest price advanced among sellers. Transactions continue subsequently until a point is reached where declining willingness to pay meets minimum accepted sales price. That's the market equilibrium for the product at hand and the market price.

Consider now what may be called a *market of convictions* (Kroman 2013; Kroman Dahl and Hendricks 2014). Let *opinion* denote the liquidity the individual may invest and let *conviction* denote the asset (that you may invest in). There are many convictions you may invest your opinion in (political, religious, social, scientific, fashionable . . . convictions) but assume for simplicity, and to meet the condition of homogeneity, that there is market for every conviction and that the (sub)population may either support the conviction or not—thus, for or against the "Stand your ground" law, say, would serve as an example. To further idealize, assume that there is equal access to arguments for or against the conviction in question discounting immediate polarization, social influence and other crowd bias-inducing phenomena.

Supply on the market of convictions is given by who may be convinced to invest their opinion in a conviction and their threshold for tipping accordingly. The ones who attempt to persuade the supply of "convincibles" provide the *demand*. A conviction is not something in demand and then purchased but something to be persuaded of. You invest your opinion in a conviction because somebody persuaded or convinced you to do so. People invest their singular opinion to convince other individuals in the population. The number of convinced will be determined by considering the number of convinced as a function of their individual thresholds for tipping and the number of convinced as a function of persuasiveness among the "sellers". In line with classical economic theory, the one who convinces the best will do so to the one who is easiest to persuade. So it will continue until equilibrium is reached between the numbers of convinced parties the market can take at a given demand for "convincibles".

Assets may overheat on the market of convictions in a way similar to overexposed assets in finance. The fundamental value of the asset on the market of convictions is given by the amount of information required to convince a population. The fundamental value is not some fixed price but rather the measure of conviction pertaining to the stance present in the population. The demand in turn becomes the number of arguments and amount of truthful information the market can muster pertaining to the conviction discounting wrongful information and cognitive bias. This latter criterion of discounting wrongful information and cognitive bias is to line up with the classical economic model revealing the largest number of transactions to the best price on the market. On the market of convictions the fundamental value is determined by the number of people who have invested their opinion in the conviction given truthful information on the market.

When people are persuaded, it may due to either supply or demand. When people are persuaded of a certain conviction due to supply the thresholds of tipping among the members of the population have lowered. On the demand side, an increase in the number of opinions on the market may press the number of persuaded parties given social proof, cascades, polarization, echo-chambers, bandwagons, boom-thinking and other factors, having nothing to do with the fundamental value of the asset or conviction.

When an individual opinion investor has to assess the market to see whether it is worth investing an opinion, *all* the information must be considered to determine the fundamental value of the asset. But true as well as false information is on the market about the *actual* distribution of devotion to the conviction in question and why. The demand side may include both true and false information possibly elevating the fundamental value of the conviction for the wrong reasons. If it becomes clear that people mostly subscribe to the conviction due to social proof or social influence bias rather than personal preferences, convincing arguments and truthful information the bubble may burst or deflate just like in finance.

The easy way to register subscription, or the easy way to invest your opinion in some conviction on social media, is via "likes" or upvotes. Now, "likes" or upvotes are risk-minimal, or non-risk, premiums and don't necessarily in any way reflect part of the fundamental value of subscribing to some conviction—you risk little by pressing "like", but you don't necessarily get much back either.

But you may get something back: Bubbles are not by definition malignant if they adequately mirror public conviction on correct information and where social influence rails rationality and reason rather than irresolution and rashness. Bubbles emerging calling for crowd climate awareness, race and gender equality, abolishment of tyrannies etc. for sure seem benign.

7.6 Noise Traders and Noisemakers

Perhaps incorrect information, rumors, hoaxes, hoodwinks and hearsays bamboozling financial markets are inevitable—from the Weidmann rumor on "Russian Markets" to the Associated Press hoax tweet concerning the White House attack. Perhaps this sort of *noise* is even necessary for trading.

The famous American economist and former President of the American Finance Association, Fisher Black (1938–1995), has argued that some traders, known as *noise traders*, act on mistaken or incorrect information and feel overly confident that this information gives them an edge although it is in fact a false sense of security. Even more alarming is Black's idea that "noise trading is essential to the existence of liquid markets" and "noise makes financial markets possible, but also makes them imperfect" (Black 1985, p. 529).

Now, if markets were informationally efficient, in the sense that everybody have access to, and act on, correct information, there would be no such thing as profitable trading, and so trading would stop. If traders won't trade, the market will no longer be liquid. That would be the end of it; "stock prices will cease to be informative; society will misallocate its scare capital." (Becker 2004, p. 15). Thus, markets must suffer from imperfection. Not all traders can be well-informed—that's the source of imperfect markets. Information is cheap and ready available but some traders mistake noise for information, and act on the former only to become noise traders according to Black. This very feature of human habitus (and thus the existence of liquidity or noise traders) is a prerequisite for trade to take place at all. One may amplify this unfortunate habitus by information technology to the point where even trade algorithms become noise traders. That's "disconcerting" as Tom Hanks says in "Saving Private Ryan" while a German moral officer under attack by Hanks' platoon over a speaker system yells that "the Statue of Liberty is kaput!"

Noise traders are apparently necessary for financial markets; perhaps *noisemakers* are likewise necessary for opinion markets, crowd-based opinion aggregators and the blogosphere to work at all? Black seems to positively anticipate this framed in terms of the stock-like dynamics of human capital:

> I suspect that if it were possible to observe the value of human capital, we would find it fluctuating in much the same way that the level of the stock market fluctuates. In fact, I think we would find fluctuations in the value of human capital to be highly correlated with fluctuations in the level of the stock market, though the magnitude of fluctuations in the value of human capital is probably less than the magnitude of the fluctuations in the level of the stock market. (Black 1985, p. 536)

"The 29 Stages of a Twitterstorm" were recently documented by BuzzFeed[7] (Fig. 7.1). Quite some witness to fluctuations of the value of human capital and noisemaking resulting in infostorms generating opinion bubbles:

The smart money often enough drives out the dumb money in finance—sophisticated traders who have adequate information and rational expectations correctly balancing asset price with its fundamental value in the end drive out the noise traders because of their informational misconceptions and false beliefs about some risky asset's price and the underlying financial instrument's fundamental value (Becker 2004, p. 16).

Noisemakers on opinion markets, in the blogosphere and on social media may fuel the fire of heated debate and facilitate exchanges of opinions. Bubbles of

---

[7] Phillips, T. (2013). "The 29 Stages of a Twitterstorm", BuzzFeed, posted October 11, http://www.buzzfeed.com/tomphillips/the-29-stages-of-a-twitterstorm, accessed October 22, 2013.

```
 1.  Somebody, somewhere does something bad.
 2.  Somebody spots the bad thing.
 3.  At first, people mostly just think it's a bit
     weird.
 4.  But gradually, the anger builds…
 5.  …and builds…
 6.  …and builds…
 7.  …and builds.
 8.  Famous Twitter users with large followings start to
     retweet it. It has now reached a tipping point and
     cannot be stopped.
 9.  People start sending angry messages to the wrong
     Twitter account.
10.  Somebody starts a petition.
11.  Somebody else starts another petition.
12.  There are now lots of petitions. Nobody is entirely
     sure which petition to sign.
13.  People start doing satire about it.
14.  Some people try to calm things down a little bit.
     It doesn't go well.
15.  The issue makes it onto the trending list.
16.  The media starts to cover the story.
17.  A boycott is suggested.
18.  Politicians jump on the bandwagon.
19.  People start using the bad thing as an excuse to
     talk about their own pet issues. Again.
20.  Somebody writes a defence of the people who did the
     bad thing.
21.  People coming to it late desperately try to work
     out what's happened.
22.  The story starts to dominate the media.
23.  Focusing on the key issue, social media "experts"
     rub their hands with glee at a new case study to
     write about.
24.  Eventually, after hours of silence, the people who
     did the bad thing apologize. To everybody. At once.
25.  And even though it's not a very good apology, it
     seems to defuse the situation just enough that the
     Twitterstorm starts to die down.
26.  Until the next day a celebrity who's only just seen
     it and can't be bothered to check what the outcome
     was starts the whole thing up again.
27.  Fortunately, at this point somebody invents a
     hashtag game and everybody gets distracted.
28.  And eventually, everything calms down and returns
     to normal.
29.  But then the next day, somebody, somewhere does
     something bad…
     … and the Circle of Life can begin once again.
```

Fig. 7.1 The 29 stages of a Twitterstorm

opinions, or conviction peaks, may grow accordingly for or against a certain company, person, position, policy, stance or viewpoint without necessarily reflecting real personal preference or the true distribution of different convictions in a population. The fundamental value of the conviction as an asset is, roughly speaking, given by the right reasons for investing your opinion assuming there are such. If it becomes clear that noise and social proof are responsible for aligned convictions rather than correct information and convincing arguments—and there's no new (junk) evidence forthcoming to fuel the fire—the bubble may deflate or the (Twitter-)storm die out. Until next time—and noisemakers start up another cycle.

Chapter 8
Lethal Logic

> *To pull our soldiers back home now is possibly the most stupid*
> *thing we can do. Our fallen brothers will be in vain. We can*
> *withdraw our soldiers as soon as our objective has been*
> *accomplished. Just so we know that our soldiers haven't died in*
> *vain.*

—Comment on YouTube

8.1 Just Another Day at the Office

You probably don't remember what you were doing on April 22nd 2009. We do. What otherwise started out as a perfectly ordinary Friday morning at the office took a sudden turn when the phone on Vincent's side of the desk rang. It was a call from The Danish Army Operational Command. In a brief conversation Vincent was told that his brother, who served as a first lieutenant in Afghanistan, had been hit by an IED (Improvised Explosive Device), while attempting to rescue one of his troops a short distance from their patrol base. His condition was critical.

In the blink of an eye, while the coffee machine was brewing leisurely and Pelle was battling with mathematical auction theory on his side of the desk, Vincent was thrown into a situation that so many relatives have experienced or feared every day, ever since the US and its allies went to war in the Middle East following the terrorist attacks on September 11, 2001; a situation where wider political decisions about events unfolding thousands of miles away have a direct impact on our personal lives and families. Fortunately Vincent's brother survived (and actually later went back to re-join his squad in Afghanistan to finish the tour). Not everyone has been so fortunate, though. By August 2013 the number of coalition casualties in Afghanistan reached 3358[1]—and for every day that passes, that number is only bound to increase.

In the wake of what happened that morning, we began to discuss various aspects of the war more often. A natural consequence was that we started to apply the tools of logic and decision-theory to elements of the public debate concerning the war effort and the reasoning patterns underlying this. Following the news we found it particularly interesting how the death tolls continuously were—and still are—used both as part of arguments to pull out and as part of arguments in support for the continuation of the war effort. A particular widespread and powerful argument, it seems, is that the thousands of lives mirrored in the death toll will have be ı lost in

---

[1] http://icasualties.org/oef/, accessed August 15, 2013.

V. F. Hendricks, P. G. Hansen, *Infostorms*, DOI 10.1007/978-3-319-03832-2_8,
© Springer International Publishing Switzerland 2014

vain if the coalition is to pull out. So one recurrent question to us became: *What part, if any, should the death tolls play in our reasoning about a continued involvement in wars like that in Afghanistan?*

Little did we expect that the answer was to be found in the logic of the kind of auction theory that Pelle was working on that morning, combined with the psychology playing out at bus stops just outside our homes. After all, there seems to be a world of difference between the events unfolding in Afghanistan, the auctions on iPhones and kitchen equipment found on the Internet, and waiting in the rain for the next city bus. Yet, it turns out phenomena like these share fundamental decision structures and psychological mechanisms, which not only leave their mark on the debate concerning our involvement in foreign wars, but also on a long line of more or less important decisions in our everyday lives.

8.2   Quicksand at the Bus Stop

The beginning of an answer to our question about the legit role of death tolls started to appear to us following an event that occurred repeatedly at the office. At that time Pelle would over and again arrive at work rain-soaked from top to toe. This despite the fact that getting to work only involved a short trip on the bus to the Central Station to catch the train to the university on the outskirts of Copenhagen. Unfortunately for Pelle, though, the buses in his neighborhood were notoriously difficult to predict. The long, yellow coaches were prone to get caught in rush hour traffic, and even worse he often ended up watching on helplessly while one overloaded bus passed by after another—and this particularly appeared to happen whenever it rained!

When dry it doesn't take long to identify the reason why rain correlates with waiting time at the bus stop. For quite obvious reasons the waiting time in public city traffic often depends more on the weather than the bus-schedule: The worse the weather, the more appealing the idea of a warm and dry bus appears relative to travelling by alternative means such as on foot or by bike. As a consequence more people will line up at bus stops when it rains, which in turn means that buses will fill quickly, which in turn causes more buses to pass, thereby creating longer waiting times and queuing for people standing in the rain further down the street.

Now, of course, if we had written Chap. 2 of this book at that time, Pelle might have been less likely to ever end up waiting in line at the bus stop when it rains. We would have been able to more easily recognize the causal chain of events just described as well as recognize that a long line of people at the bus stop does not necessarily provide one with any good reason for believing that there are many buses on the street that day or that there is a bus coming just around the corner. Rather it may imply quite the opposite. Still, even then, people like us who ordinarily conduct research on information phenomena such as pluralistic ignorance and informational cascades, easily get fooled by a little complexity, especially in seemingly trivial contexts and situations. When first fallen into the trap, we, like everybody else, tend to get stuck in the much more devastating trap: *The quicksand at the bus stop.*

The quicksand at the bus stop is a metaphor for the following well-known situation: You have lined up at the bus stop, in spite of the destination being within such easy reach that you might as well walk. As time passes without any sign of the bus you soon begin to consider whether it was actually a good decision to line up at the bus stop in the first place. This thought is followed by the idea that perhaps it would still pay off just to walk. As the minutes pass in the rain, it begins to dawn on you that if you had chosen to walk or take the bike, you would in all likelihood already have reached your destination. So, really, wouldn't it be most sensible to just grab your bag and walk off?

But just when you think of moving, the following train of thought forms which has the effect of holding you back: The bus *must* be on its way. After all, you have waited for a long time now. Further, imagine if you walked off just to see the bus pass by after you had walked only 50 yards—what vexation! Regret is a terrible and powerful feeling. Finally, the moment you decide to throw in the towel and walk, you will have to accept that the time you have been waiting was a wait in vain. Such deliberation not only ends up tying you to the bus stop; deliberation also takes time, and the longer you stand there and think about it, the more you appear to lose by abandoning the plan and taking off on foot. Slowly but surely, you reason your way deeper and deeper into the quicksand at the bus stop. Like everyone else you stand and wait... and wait... and wait... until a bus finally arrives and brings you to work soaked. You then have to explain why you were *once again* late because you carefully thought about how to optimize at each step of the journey. At least that is what so often happened to Pelle during that spring.

8.3   The Logic of Death Tolls

So what does all this have to do with Afghanistan? Is there quicksand for our decisions only to suck us in deeper here too? Is it possible that the same train of thought, which left us standing in the rain at the bus stop, is also part of maintaining the pressure for a continued involvement in war efforts in a country far, far away? There is much to be said in support of this.

Take for instance John Bolton, the former US ambassador to the UN. In support of a continued involvement he stated the following on the Fox News program "On the record" on October 9th 2012:

> In fact, I think it's almost inevitable that if we withdraw from Afghanistan—according to the President's schedule in 2014—that the Taliban and Al Qaeda are gonna take back over again and this human sacrifice we've made—2,000 Americans dead—will have been completely wasted.

Similar versions of this argument can be found in blogs and commentaries all over the Internet. For instance one can find similar comments on YouTube in abundance:

> To pull our soldiers back now is possibly the most stupid thing you can do. Then our fallen brothers will be in vain. We can withdraw our soldiers as soon as our objective has been accomplished. Just so we know that our soldiers haven't died in vain.

What should strike you about this train of reasoning is that it is virtually identical to the deliberations, which we experience at the bus stop. That is, if we leave Afghanistan (or the bus stop), the soldiers who lost their lives (or the time invested in waiting) have lost their lives in vain (or is wasted in vain). Thus just as the fear of having waited in vain at the bus stop renders it difficult to walk away, the fear of the soldiers having died in vain makes the decision to forsake our involvement in Afghanistan hard. And obviously it only adds to the problem that comprehensive social pressures kick in when such a decision is a political one and considerations take place in public debate. Imagine yourself explaining your decision to pull the troops out to the relatives of those who have died. How would you ever go about explaining the wives, mothers, fathers, siblings and children left behind, that their father, husband, son, brother, mother, wife, daughter or sister died in vain in a country thousands of miles away? It's tragic, but it seems difficult, if not impossible, to ever escape this lethal logic of the death tolls when in the spotlight of the public sphere.

With regard to the death tolls in Afghanistan then, the result seems to inevitably be that pondering the problem further will—like at the bus stop—simply cause you to sink further into quicksand. Regardless of whether or not you should have stayed away in the first place, the sad truth is that once you're there, you stay and fight. If you throw in the towel and leave Afghanistan, wouldn't the young soldiers' lives have been wasted? And what's worse, what if we are that close to making it? If, like the bus just around the corner, the war in Afghanistan is on the brink of a critical turning point, where our luck will turn and become better day-by-day? And what's more, keep in mind that this is a case of life and death rather than just entering the office with wet socks. To anyone who remembers the pictures from the national stadium in Kabul it's clear that it is not just a warm and dry bus or political pride which is at stake—it is the safety, lives and wellbeing of Afghani fathers, and especially mothers and children as well as thousands of young soldiers.

In conclusion, the parallel between the bus stop and the involvement in Afghanistan serves to explain how we reason about death tolls relative to our continuous involvement. Still, there's something uncomfortable about this way of reasoning. In particular, there seems to be no end to the costs that one should be willing to incur, nor any solution to be found in the parallel—and that seems puzzling if not worrying, to say the least. Thus the question arises whether there are any bounds of reason in the structure underlying this 'lethal logic' of the death tolls. Is the underlying thinking really as rationally sound and sensible as it seems, or does it ultimately rest on some fallacy of reasoning? Can we ever escape the conclusion? To answer these questions we need to move even further away from war-torn zones and into our lectures on rationality in action and epistemic logic that usually take place in calm lecture halls at universities far removed from any real action.

8.4   Taking a Hammering at the Auction

Once, teaching his course 'Rationality in Action', Pelle had the idea of paying students a wage for coming to class. It was however neither a cunning trick devised to spur the participation of sleepy students, or to compensate them for the additional hours he usually requires them to put in. Rather it was an attempt to make one of the course's centrepieces pertaining to the pitfalls of rational deliberation comprehensible in practise.

The study of rational deliberation and action falls within classical philosophy as well as modern microeconomics. A special branch of this is called *game theory* (which we have already mentioned in previous chapters). Game theory considers what happens when several rational agents interact, or when a rational agent simulates the interdependency of multiple agents' decision making prior to making a choice. In recent years research within this field has won distinction and led to several Nobel Laureates in Economics such as Robert Aumann and Thomas Schelling. The research has also been put to practical use in public invitations to the corporate sector to tender auctions, as well as applied in the analysis of collective action, or lack thereof, such as that involved in the case of global warming, over-fishing and traffic jams (Chap. 4).

The first exercise Pelle exposed the students to after they had received 500 chips just for turning up was the so-called *dollar auction*. This exercise is a *game* that's a standard introductory example invented by the game theorist Martin Shubik. It is usually employed to demonstrate to students how much trouble even sensible people can easily get themselves into when they are left in a thoroughly manipulated situation.

The rules of the dollar auction are relatively simple: A seller puts an item up for auction that the participants at the auction can subsequently choose to bid for or not. In class, where transparency is a virtue, Pelle as the supplier of the auction puts up 100 chips. Participants then bid and as in most other auctions the highest bidder receives the item by paying his highest bid. The only 'small' difference in this type of auction compared to other auctions is that *everyone* placing a bid must pay the supplier for their heighest bid To some this rule is perhaps a bit strange, but as Pelle is quick to point out it is nevertheless just an auction. Concerned more with the possible gains the students usually take little notice of this feature. Well, at least until they all too late discover that they have been had. This happens only a few minutes later when the one who wins the auction usually has to pay around 350–450 chips for the 100 chips while Pelle on the other hand walks happily out of the door with up to 3000–4000 chips and debt certificates that may be redeemed by substitution assignments.

Now one might think that today's university students must be uncommonly dense. Not so of course. The problem is rather that they are a bit too eager to apply their rational skills. It only requires a little elementary school mathematics to see why.

For pragmatic considerations assume that one can only choose between bidding 10 chips more than the last bid, or refrain from bidding. When the auction starts, each student can therefore choose to refrain from bidding, which gives him an outcome of zero chips, or to bid 10 chips, which promises him $100 - 10 = 90$ chips if no one else bids. Choosing between respectively 0 or 90 chips isn't difficult. When readily applied reason therefore dictates that each student bid, if no one else does. When the first bid has fallen, the remaining students' choice then stands between bidding 20 chips or refrain from bidding, i.e. a choice between 0 or 80 chips. Once again, the only rational thing to do is to bid for the 100 chips. When the bid of 20 chips has fallen, the logic remains the same—only the choice is now between 0 or 70 chips to those who are yet to place their first bid, and between − 10 and 70 to the first who placed a bid (remember, the outcome − 10 is due to the nature of auction; one will ultimately have to pay ones highest bid regardless of whether one wins the auction or not). Those who placed a bid in the beginning also have the strongest incentive to continue bidding, since they otherwise lose what they have already bid.

This is where things get ugly and everything ends in a collective disaster. No matter how many times one is outbid, the rational action is to continue bidding –in the beginning with the anticipation of landing a profit rather than a loss, but soon, solely with the aim of minimizing the obvious catastrophe. For instance, if you end up being the one who bid 80 for a 100 chips, you still stand to win 20. But of course the person who bid 70 will now bid 90 chips to win 10 instead of losing 70 chips she otherwise stands to lose. If you are next in line you are left with the choice between accepting a point-blank loss of 80 chips or bid the damn 100 chips for the self-same 100 chips and thereby at least be allowed to withdraw with no skin off your nose. But as soon as you bid a 100, the one who bid 90 stands with the choice between − 90 (i.e. quitting) or − 10 chips, i.e. bidding 110 chips for 100 chips! Once again reason dictates your opponent to bid, even though the cost of bidding has now exceeded the prize of 100 chips which the auction offers. It is the only way to reduce the loss. When doing so, you face the choice between -100 chips, or bidding 120 chips for 100 chips resulting in − 20 . . . so what to do? This logic continues forever and many of the students play along right up until they run out of chips and Pelle happily starts to lend them more. Counterintuitive? Yes. Irrational? Not in the least—at least not when viewed in isolation.

8.5   A Lemon Market for Apples

Of course, class auctions with chips as prizes are artificial. So does similar decision making occur with real money? Do people really fall for such a trick? Most sensible people normally say that they would never place a bid at a dollar auction. But unfortunately actions speak louder than words. Experiments confirm that if the right item appears for auction –an iPhone, a fashionable pair of shoes, or whatever turns you on—most people begin to bid. When they see that no one else is bidding, they think it would be stupid not to place a bid themselves. These experiments also show that once we have walked into the bear trap, we all tend to get stuck even though we soon recognize the nature of our predicament. Finally, such experiments point to the fact that people will not stop until they have reached a mental ceiling, the nature of which of course varies from subject to subject. For some it's the psychological shift from the chase of a prize to the minimization of a loss, others react to other people's reproachful looks and laughter and for yet others it's the appearance of an empty wallet. Evidence points to the former of these possibilities as having the least influence, and the latter as making the biggest dent.

Turning to the world outside experiments the evidence becomes even stronger. In the real world the practical counterparts to the dollar auction are not easily recognized—yet the consequences are still real. When you have lined up at the bus stop in the first place, it becomes harder and harder to leave, since you have already invested your time waiting. When presidents and generals invade countries it gradually becomes harder and harder to pull out as the death toll rises. Do they really want to be blamed for young people losing their lives in vain? No, and history shows that they are not alone. In a complex decision environment when stakes are harder to quantify the logic seems more inevitable than any other place. And when it comes to improving our decisions in these situations the prospect is bleak. Experience and improvement of performance don't readily follow as long as we do not discover the recurring structure of the predicament.

A most startling case of real world evidence of this phenomenon is found in the so-called *penny-auctions* on the Internet. In such auctions consumers are offered 'bidding packages' consisting of bidding tickets, which have a unit price between a dollar and 70 cents depending on how many tickets are bought at a time. One may then subsequently place a bid on an iPhone, a flat screen, a camera or other electronics by putting one of the tickets down for the item. The person to place the last ticket before the deadline wins the right to purchase the item at a bargain price. This bargain price begins at $ 0 and every time a bid ticket is added onto the pile, the price you are allowed to buy the product for only raises $ 0.17. So if you are the last to place a bid and for instance number 5 placing a ticket, you might actually get to buy an iPhone 5 which runs at $ 849, for only $ 0.7 + (5 x $ 0.17) = $ 1.55! What is especially attractive about this kind of auction is the special "the one who placed the last bid" variation. This creates the possibility that one may only have to put a single ticket down after a 1000 other participants have placed a bid, and still win the right to buy the item auctioned off at $ 170. In principle there is a real possibility of making a really good deal (but notice that in this case the auctioneer makes at least $ 700 + $ 170 = $ 870, and 999 people may pay $ 0.7 for nothing).

These subtle changes don't alter the fact that the penny-auction's fundamental logic is identical to that of a dollar auction: *Once you have placed the first bid, rationality seems to dictate that you continue the bidding.* If you have bid once, you have already invested at least $ 0.7, which you will otherwise lose. The only relevant difference created by the Internet auctions' introduction of bidding tickets is that even new arrivals find it appealing to join the hoax (without realizing, of course, that it's a hoax). In the lecture hall new arrivals would not find it attractive to bid on 100 chips once the highest bid has passed 90 chips, not to say reached around 2–300 chips. But, the ticket scheme combined with the incremental rise in price acts to hide the collective consequences as participants keep on bidding up the items. That is, contrary to the class auction the true costs for consumers are not reflected in the price as the price merely increases $ 0.17 per bid placed.

This business model is stretched to its full potential. Thus another additional feature added by the penny-auctions on the Internet is that of extending deadlines when a bid is placed within the very last minutes. Surely this is only good business 'ethics', since it provides other participants with the opportunity to renew their bids—in fact, even if other participants don't renew, many users as well as consumer protection agencies have pointed out that the auction houses will extend the auction anyway by putting in bids themselves. In this way, the kind of money that some of the Internet penny-auctions ultimately get away with is guaranteed to be far more than just the 2 or 3 times the product's value or recommended retail price, that Pelle gets away with in class. It's thus not a market for lemons, but the market is a lemon itself.

8.6 Zombies in Vegas

Despite the nature of these penny-auctions, consumer authorities across the world have had severe difficulties in deciding whether they should be regarded as legal. Examining the penny-auctions carefully, it's evident that they haven't been designed to perfect the market-mechanism which auctions are usually designed to serve.

What normally characterizes an auction is the mechanism that essentially generates the bid, which corresponds to the highest personal appraisal of the item's value amongst the auction's participants (or second highest, depending of the auction type). In a regular auction an item or service is put up for auction, and the auction mechanism then sees to it that the person who values the item most is the one who also gets it. The auction provider is given a good price for the item auctioned—even if this is rare and thus the value of the item is difficult to determine—and the bidding scheme is 'fair' to those who are interested in bidding (given that one assumes that the distribution of money that participants have in their pockets is considered as fair). This is seen in game theory, where the price brought about by such a mechanism is referred to as the 'solution'. Generally speaking, the solution to a real auction is that everyone always bids up to the value, which reflects how much they value the item, but usually only up until everyone else stops bidding. It's precisely therefore, that a winner of a standard auction ends up paying the second highest valuation of the item's value when bids are made in turns and as common knowledge. The rationale behind this solution is, that if you bid less than your personal valuation, you will regret it when someone outbids you; and if you bid more than your personal valuation, you'll regret it if you win. Auctions are thus characterized by the fact that the best strategy for all is to bid up to the amount, which corresponds to their personal valuation of the auction item's value. Hence, auctions are a simple distribution and price coordination device giving the auction provider the (second) best possible price, while also giving the item to the person who values it the most.

In light of this, it's also evident why the dollar auction in class and the penny-auctions on the Internet do not trivially qualify as auctions. These auctions do not provide a mechanism that readily generates the highest price for the provider relative to the participants' personal valuation of the item. In the classroom situation the students actually end up bidding more than a 100 chips for a 100 chips –100 chips can't be worth more than 100 chips. In the dollar auction, so far described, there seems to be no such thing as a solution in the game. Reason begs you to continue bidding, right up until something or someone stops you. The dollar auction's way of working with our psychology is thus *to put rational actions into overdrive instead of coordinating them.*

Likewise the penny-auctions on the Internet are deliberately designed to hoodwink the consumer, so as to undermine the coordinating function of the auction mechanism. If standard auctions resembled penny-auctions in general, auctions would have been banned long ago. For just as Ulysses wished to be tied to the mast to counter the siren's song, it's only natural for people to decide to prevent themselves from omitting foolish mistakes, when they are otherwise able to see through them. Moreover, there is no practical problem in a prospective legislation which forbids such scam-auctions. An auction's effectiveness as a price coordination device may be empirically measured relative to its mathematically well-defined game theoretic solution. Obviously, the observed behaviour in dollar and penny-auctions where consumers pay far more than they value the item up for auction, systematically and intentionally obstructs effective coordination. A direct ban of penny-auctions based on empirical performance tests is of course difficult. But fortunately there is another solution. Since regret is a natural result of participating in a penny-auction, the easiest way to regulate them is by introducing consumer rights to regret the purchase of the bidding-tickets offered by these auctions. This was done in Denmark, and soon most of the penny-auctions had to close down.

Alternatively, consumer authorities could also decide that the dollar auctions on the Internet should be prohibited to call themselves auctions in favour of what they truly are in practice: *One-armed bandits.* The practical logic followed by participants is actually the same. When you throw the first coin into the gaping slot of a one-armed bandit, it is naturally in hope of winning the grand prize. The wheel spins again and again in vain, but with the small twist that applies to one-armed bandits; a little bait is payed out at intervals timed to match human impatience. The hope of the quick grand prize, however, dwindles in line with the money, only to be replaced with the wish to recover what is lost. Zombies in front of the one-armed bandits in Las Vegas, as well as down on the corner in the local gaming club, bear all too clear witness to how hypnotic the death toll's logic can be when our focus becomes fixed on the ever-spinning wheel.

8.7 Escaping the One-Armed Bandit in Afghanistan

The purpose here is not to take a stand on what legal actions consumer agencies should pursue or the legitimacy of the continued international involvement in Afghanistan and elsewhere. Instead we will simply take a closer look at the fundamental psychology of the *one-armed bandit,* and rightly so. This psychology not only leaves its stamp on the debate and the decisions regarding the continuance of our involvement, but also on a long line of other more or less important decisions in everyday life; decisions ranging all the way from the bus stop to buying a cell phone on the Internet. Intriguingly, it appears that the reasoning it provokes is actually both rational and logical if one is narrowly focused on the spinning wheel. So where does this leave us? Are we all doomed to sink ever deeper into the death toll's literally lethal logic, or is there a way out, disarming the biased focus on what has already been lost?

Realize initially that it's no use just wiping the slate clean and starting over as is sometimes suggested in the economic literature as well as by common sense. It is easy to see why. If we return to the students in the class auction we observe that even if a student chooses to regard the, say 200 chips, he has bid in the last bidding round as a sunken cost, it doesn't save him from the wretched affair. It just means that once again it will only take 10 chips to place a bid on the 100 chips. Therefore it becomes rational to bid anew, since the loss doesn't amount to -200 chips, but returns to 0 why bidding up 10 again becomes a gain of $-10 + 100 = 90$. Forgive and forget, then, doesn't work. This shows that if we are to escape the one-armed bandit in Afghanistan (as well as the time lost, if we wish to escape the quicksand at the bus stop) we are bound to maintain the death toll as a central element in our decision making.

Likewise realize that it's not just a lack of information that creates the problem. Again the evidence is found by considering the students playing the auction game. They were aware of the rules of the auction, including the number of chips which they were given, aware that the highest bidder would receive the 100 chips for his or her highest bid, as well as that everyone must pay their highest bid, *even* if they didn't win the auction. The same seems to go for the participants on the Internet's penny-auctions and the people lining up at the bus stop.

But couldn't one raise the objection here that they didn't know or weren't capable of following the logic to its conclusion? What if they had become aware of this, if they had been informed of all that has been discussed in this chapter up until now? Wouldn't they have refrained from bidding?

Unfortunately, this does not seem to be the case. Even when Pelle plays the auction again with the students, shortly after they have seen the result in practise and had the logic explained to them, surprisingly many bid again. As stated earlier, the students are anything but dumb. They simply just don't differ from those who once again line up at the bus stop, or those who decide to bid yet again on the Internet auction. They are actually caught in a simple trap. A sound argument must end with one of the two following conclusions: either (1) that it's not rational to place a bid, or (2) that it is rational to place a bid. But if they, based on the information regarding the death toll's logic, can soundly deduce (1), that one shouldn't place a bid, then no one will bid. But that's exactly when it's sensible to bid, precisely because no one else is doing it! Hence: The conclusion can only be (2) that it's sensible to place a bid.

A third possibility was touched upon above in relation to the Internet auctions. One could simply choose to ban one-armed bandits. That's at any rate the solution the University has promised to enforce, in case Pelle should ever consider using real money in the auctions during his lessons. But once again, it's relatively easy to see why such a solution wouldn't be particularly efficient in every respect. What is it exactly, for instance, that one is supposed to forbid pertaining to bus stops? That people line up and wait? That probably wouldn't be advisable. And how about the war in Afghanistan? Here the problem is—as is often the case in love and war—that there is no third party who can enforce a collective desirable solution. In the end it may therefore be concluded that a ban does not constitute a sustainable solution, whether concerning Zombies in front of the one-armed bandits in Las Vegas, the quicksand at the bus stop, or the death toll's lethal logic in Afghanistan.

Finally, while the solution of regretting the purchase works beautifully for the penny-auctions on the Internet, it has no parallel outside the auction room. Time at the bus stop is a one-way ticket, and death gives no refunds. But does this really mean that we are forever bound to the one-armed bandit, as soon as we have invested the first coin?

8.8   In the Pocket of the Taliban

If there exists a sensible way out of Afghanistan, it can only be because something has been overlooked. This is however not so strange, since it appears that the way is concealed at exactly the moment one begins focusing on the death toll's logic. The pivot of the death toll's logic is built upon limited focus on what is lost, and what can be gained, respectively. The way out therefore consists in implicating a third element: What Taliban has in its pockets.

To understand this we turn to the dollar auction with the students for the last time. Imagine that there are only two students, of whom one has 50 chips, while the other only has 40 chips. One rarely has the exact same resources at ones disposal. This circumstance adds both a new and obvious solution to the problem. If the two students have seen through the death toll's logic, and their disposable income is *common knowledge* (Cf. Chap. 3), they will now be able to reason as follows: They know that if neither of them places a bid, it's rational for them both to bid. But it's also apparent to both of them that the student who has 50 chips in his pocket ultimately will win the auction and thereby gain $100 - 50 = 50$ chips. The student with 40 chips can therefore choose to participate in the auction with the certainty of losing somewhere between 10 and 40 chips or refuse to participate. With this focus on the *relative difference* in chips instead of just on what's lost and what may be won, it's therefore rational for the one who has most chips to place a bid. This solution applies to all uneven distributions of chips where one student has less than the other. With focus on the relative difference in resources, the way out of the death toll's logic may be found.

The only problem is that one rarely knows what ones 'opponent' has in his pocket, let alone it being common knowledge. In that case it's only sensible to participate in the auction, as long as you think that there is a certain likelihood of you being willing to pay the highest price. This also applies to the involvement in Afghanistan. The problem is however, that there must be two parties to make a war. Thus Taliban must also be thinking that there is some certain likelihood that they are willing to pay a higher price than their opponents. The obvious problem, though, is that both parties cannot in the end be correct in believing that they are the ones who are willing to pay most.

The central element therefore becomes: One mustn't overlook reality's indicators of who is willing to pay the most. These indicators must not be overlooked since the lack of common knowledge is precisely why it's solely these indicators—which occasion adjustment of the probability—on which the parties valuate that they each will win in the end. Once one has learned to focus on these indicators, it subsequently follows that as soon as one finds it predominantly likely that one's opponent is willing to go further than oneself, one should pull out without glancing at what has been lost. It's therefore the *relative willingness* and *these indicators* rather than the *death toll's logic* which should be focused on if reason is to guide us when we are faced with the one-armed bandit in Afghanistan. Any reference to the death toll's logic in the debate concerning international involvement must be characterized as a lack of sense of direction. It's use in the debate is the rhetorical attempt of a penny-auction. A sensible way out of Afghanistan must instead be based on what we are willing to sacrifice for an entire nation's welfare and safety—otherwise, our soldiers will have died in vain.

Chapter 9
Simply Wrong

Everything must be made as simple as possible. But not simpler.

—Albert Einstein

The discussion of framing effects in Chaps. 5 and 8 showed that the frame or perspective applied to a given problem crucially effects individual decisions and actions. Parts of a decision frame affect us in subtle psychological ways that shouldn't make any difference in principle, but nevertheless do so as a matter of fact—for instance, the ordering of a set of choices or the formulation of choice options. Other parts of a decision frame affect choices due to the selection of what information is identified as relevant to decisions. Should you keep waiting for the bus, or keep bidding on the cell phone? Well, the decision depends on what information you take into account as relevant—in particular, on whether you only pay attention to your own losses as they occur, or plan relative in advance to risks and your opponents' resources (see Chap. 8).

This latter aspect of framing implies that some frames or models of our choice predicaments are better fit to reach our purposes and solve our problems than others. If you ignore relevant information things may turn out badly. Remember Chaps. 2 and 3 demonstrated how too much and too little information may lead us astray and away from our goals. Decision theorists and game theorists refer to this problem of determining the relevant information as constructing 'the right model or game' of the situation. Such a construction depends both on getting the facts about the situation straight and on getting our own purposes for decision making right. But in the heat of the game we often lose sight of what we are doing. That is, in practice we often get the models wrong.

This is no less true when it comes to our everyday interactions and social institutions. As Chap. 4, for instance, stressed, in many social settings so-called 'freedom of choice' can't be reduced to maximizing the set of possible choices and then choosing freely under full information on a competitive market. Real political freedom of choice presupposes insight and freedom to personally choose or have a say about which perspectives and frames should be applied prior to one's choices as well as which values should guide this choice of frames. Under certain conditions it may be a competitive market that ensures efficiency, innovation and quality through its blind coordination of individual choices. But again this is not necessarily always so.

The *models* and decision frames we apply to our collective actions and institutions are more fundamental or *primary* to the *choices* that we make in pursuit of our

V. F. Hendricks, P. G. Hansen, *Infostorms*, DOI 10.1007/978-3-319-03832-2_9,
© Springer International Publishing Switzerland 2014

personal values and projects in social interaction. This is not to say that the collective is more important than the individual. But applying the right decision frames is primary for succeeding in our individual actions and projects. This also holds when it comes to situations involving coordinating our actions among us.

If we wish to change society for the better in light of the fundamental values we hold dear, close attention must be paid to the perspectives or decision frames we apply to societal institutions and the actions constituting them. Now we know that the most important choices we make in life don't consist in the isolated choices we make on an everyday basis, but rather on the broader decision frames selected. Yet, in the heat of politics and public debate we often lose sight of what we're doing. Attention becomes limited to information and choices that are merely instrumental to our individual long-term projects and personal interests. The danger attached to this delimitation is over-simplifying individuals, institutions and collective decision problems. Such dangers of simplification are the objects of this chapter: What happens when we devise political solutions in the belief that individual motives are always compatible with economic incentives, that larger social phenomena always represent individual motives and that furnishing each individual with a vote is all it takes to achieve true democracy.

9.1   A Pint of Blood, Please

Blood donation is a case in point with regard to simplifying our individual decision making too much. In the US, 1 out of 7 people entering hospital needs a blood transfusion. In the US alone, every 2 s someone is in need of blood. But since blood cannot be artificially produced, it has to be obtained from the veins of others. Most blood donors are unpaid volunteers who donate blood for a community supply. Blood banks and centers then see to it that *anyone* who ends up on the operating table, in an emergency room or a hemophiliac ward, will get the right type of blood in the measure necessary to survive. Around the world voluntary blood banks and centers like these are essential to secure the wellbeing of thousands of world citizens every year. However, the blood banks managing the system or institution of blood donation and transfusion have to deal with what is called a *collective action problem*.

A prerequisite for the blood banks are the millions of volunteers who register for free to regularly donate a pint of blood. No doubt, it's not particularly practical or comfortable for these millions of people to take time out to go to the hospital only to have their skin pierced by a needle and their blood drawn. The refund of a bus ticket and a banana, a soft drink or whatever small refreshment afterwards, hardly makes up for the physical discomfort and practical inconvenience. Thus, when *viewed in isolation*, any sensible person—with the exception of a masochist—would prefer to stay home and politely ignore the opportunity provided by the blood banks and centers. That is, the action 'stay home' is generally preferred to 'donate blood':

Stay home > donate blood

This general preference is independent of the actions each expects of other people. If you on the one hand expect that everyone else will happily go and donate blood, it doesn't make any difference for you if you should decide to stay home. Your contribution, anyway, would only amount to a drop in the ocean. Blood banks and the service they offer will continue to exist for you and everyone else to benefit from. On the other hand, if you expect that no one else will go and donate blood, you would probably not want to go either and the blood banks would cease to exist.[1] Finally, if you're like most other people you would prefer the general situation where blood banks exist and everyone regularly goes and donates blood, to the one where blood banks have all gone out of business. From a short-term self-interested perspective, no matter what you expect of others, it would be reasonable to stay home, although you'd prefer that everyone else had gone to donate blood. It's this situation that, somewhat simplified, may be referred to as the *Prisoner's dilemma*, though without the name, that pertained to dog owners or CO_2-emissions in previous chapters:

	Donate blood	Stay home
Donate blood	3,3	0,4
Stay home	4,0	1,1

Of course, there are lots of things that we do that we would prefer not to when viewed in isolation. Mowing the lawn, going to work, and paying taxes are but a few examples. Yet, Chap. 4 reminds us that in the *long-term* perspective doing these things anyway may serve our own self-interests.

Even a long-term perspective doesn't really explain the fairly smooth-running institution of voluntary blood donation. First of all, access to the system provided by blood banks and centers is completely independent of one's personal contribution. You don't need to be a blood donor yourself to receive the blood transfusions sponsored by the blood banks and centers. In fact, different from the monetary bank down on the corner, you wouldn't even have to 'pay back' your withdrawal. The blood banks therefore constitute what economists call a *public good*. No one is refused access to the benefit based on his or her possible lack of contribution to the system. Secondly, a single contribution again only amounts to a drop in the ocean. Whether a person gives blood or not has no impact on the availability of the public good. Of course, if everyone refrains from donating blood it will make a difference—but no single person makes a difference in and by him- or herself. The size of the good and its quality is distinct from each individual contribution. Thirdly, and finally, contributions as well as withdrawals are practically anonymous. There is no sanctioning

---

[1] One could also construct a model of the situation where the hospital would continue to offer a system for voluntary blood donation and transfusion even though almost no one participated. In that case, you could be sure that your blood would be highly appreciated by a concrete person. This description of the situation seems to be more fitting than the Prisoner's dilemma when it comes to people donating very rare blood types. In such situations your unique individual contribution would make a direct difference and hence you might actually want to go and donate your blood even though no one else wanted to. These observations would result in a somewhat different model called *Chicken* and some of the points in this chapter would look different.

system in place to put pressure on blood recipients to become future blood donors. Nor can citizens sanction each other. After all, one can't spot a non-blood donor on the street or know if someone who says he's a blood donor actually is such a person.

Given the collective action problem underlying the system of blood donation and the three features long-term interest cannot solve the collective action problem. Hence, it is hardly difficult to understand why blood banks and centers are fighting a constant battle to get people to become and remain blood donors, inasmuch as donation is based on a principle of voluntariness and anonymity. For instance, blood centers in the US often have difficulty maintaining even a three-day supply for routine transfusion demands. In the US less than 10 % of the population donates annually. In the UK the blood donation level is at meager 4 %.[2]

Sometimes blood banks run low. When this happens things may turn disastrous. This is what happened when a 31-year mom hemorrhaged after giving birth to a baby son in Glasgow in 1997. Shortly after giving birth she was rushed into emergency surgery and four units of blood were quickly administered in transfusions. As it turned out, four units weren't enough. However, it also turned out that the hospital had run out of blood. But despite calling around to get blood units from nearby infirmaries, the hospital couldn't get enough blood in time. Three hours after giving birth, the mother had suffered massive internal bleeding and her death certificate read that the main cause of the tragedy was a heart attack due to lack of blood.[3]

Every time a tragedy like this appears on the front page of the newspapers, there's a call for an intuitively attractive and simple solution to the problem faced by the institution of blood donation: Paying blood donors for their time and trouble. If people are well-informed about and value the existence of blood banks, but still don't contribute enough and often enough, the deficit of pro-social behavior must be due to the lack of individual incentives—and since the stick isn't an option, one is left with the carrot. This solution is more expensive than the current system. Proponents usually promise that in exchange we would be guaranteed a stable delivery of donor blood and market forces would quickly bring the price of donor blood down to an acceptable level—that is, the price which actually corresponds to the blood donor's time and trouble when giving blood relative to what they could otherwise have spent their time doing. The argument goes, by accepting some reasonable costs to incentivize each individual as in the game matrix above, the collective action problem would dissolve and the necessary blood donations would be obtained

Wouldn't it only be fair if fellow citizens fittingly rewarded the donors for their efforts? And why stop here? Why not use the same approach when it comes to the institutions of organ- or egg donation? This idea may at first appear simple and attractive. But if anything should be clear by now, it's that human behavior and the institutions humans comprise are far from being simple. In fact, we're often driven by such ingenious social motives and complex mechanisms that some behaviors are strictly incompatible with economic incentives.

---

[2] "56 Facts About Blood". America's Blood Centers. Retrieved 2013-01-04 and "Give Blood", NHS Blood & Transfusion. Retrieved 2013-07-14.

[3] The *Mirror*, December 9, 1997.

In 1971 the British social scientist Richard M. Titmuss wrote *The Gift Relationship: From Human Blood to Social Policy*. The book presented a direct criticism of commercial blood markets. Not only were commercial blood markets more expensive, Titmuss argued, they were also a worse system than the institution of voluntary donation found around the world. In particular, the payment for blood imposed by a commercial market introduced an economic motive to give blood—a motive which wasn't just an alternative, but also undermined the existing institution for voluntary blood donation.

To see why, Titmuss pointed out that the donors in voluntary schemes donate blood based on a desire to be, or at least appear as, good fellow citizens. Yet, the moment money becomes involved, blood donors can no longer be certain that others—as well as themselves—perceive the donation as sincere and charitable. That is, the motive to donate would become ambiguous. Because of this, Titmuss argued, introducing monetary incentives would undermine the original and charitable motive thereby making the rather uncomfortable and troublesome action of donating blood unattractive for most of the people who otherwise donate blood for free. In addition, Titmuss directed attention to other unintended consequences of a commercial blood market. Such a market, he noted, would lead to blood of poorer quality since the market forces would draw new blood donors who came mainly from underprivileged social stratums with increased risks of contagious deceases such as hepatitis. This problem would only be exacerbated by the fact that even when donors were aware of such risks, they would have an incentive to try to keep this knowledge hidden from the blood bank on a commercial blood market.

Even though Richard Titmuss' original arguments on certain points have been criticized for being too speculative and lacking hard evidence, a line of experiments and studies has since substantiated his conclusions. Experiments conducted in Sweden, where donors are typically paid, showed that more people are liable to give blood provided they aren't paid, or if the blood is donated to charitable causes (Mellström and Johannesson 2008). Furthermore, the phenomenon seems robust since similar results have been ascertained in other areas, such as for instance voluntary legal assistance (Ariely 2009).

Even though the idea of paying donors to give blood may initially sound attractive, one should be careful not to act on the intuition that the only motives that affect people can be reduced to, let alone be *combined* or *complemented* by, individualized economic motives. Pulling a costly, but simple market-based perspective or decision frame down over the existing perspective, where the institution of blood donation facilitates a charitable practice may easily have unfortunate consequences. To those citizens who voluntarily donate blood, donation isn't a simple Prisoner's dilemma. Rather it's a game, where the act of giving blood acts as a social identity marker. It's a marker that is orientated towards, and only makes sense in relation to, a social collective. That's why blood donors ultimately seem to prefer other people's recognition rather than sending an invoice. If we fail to observe the social nature of institutions like those for blood-, and organ-donation and their incompatibility with economic incentives, we would be simplifying too much and thereby be making a fatal and expensive mistake.

9.2   Inferring Micro-Motives from Macro-Behavior

The institution for blood donation is only one of society's numerous important institutions whose functional capacity is dependent on a collective or social perspective. Simplifying the underlying behavior too much may lead to the wrong kind of solutions. Yet, another danger of simplifying human behavior is inferring directly from observable macro-behavior to the motives that create these. A classical instance of this danger is found in the ever-resurfacing debates concerning the ghettoization of cities.

One hundred years ago most people around the world lived in the countryside in close-knit networks surrounded by people culturally much like themselves, but of very different ages and capabilities. The rise of the industrial era, and later information society and technology, gave rise to urbanization that radically changed this. In 1800, only 3 % of the world's population lived in urban areas. By 1900, almost 14 % were urbanites. In 1950, 30 % of the world's population resided in urban areas. In 2008, for the first time, the world's population was evenly split between urban and rural areas and in more developed nations about 74 % of the population had become urbanites. Cities have become a social space of unlimited possibilities—some good, some bad. Globalization has not only added new dynamics and strength to this development; it has also turned up a social challenge by gathering people in cities from ever more distant places and cultures.

From one perspective, cities may be viewed just as statistical coincidences arising from an almost infinite series of individual decisions within a geo-economic frame. From another perspective, cities are constitutive fundamental and some of the biggest institutions ever created by humans, where sewers, roads, parks, and public squares must be maintained; water has to be cleaned; traffic- and streetlights must be powered; car-parking must be coordinated and regulated; epidemics must be quelled; quality of served food as well as coastal defenses need checking; the police must control and be controlled; schools must be evaluated and the city courts must function— checks and balances through and through. While we rarely think of the modern city as anything but a huge collection of individuals, it's really a joint project, whose scope and complexity exceeds even the imagination of each of its citizens. So what happens to it if we accidentally pull an inexpediently simplistic perspective down over the problems that arise in the city?

9.2.1   The BlackBerry Riots

Between August 6–10, 2011 thousands of mostly young people rioted in several London boroughs. The resulting chaos generated a wave of looting, arson, street violence and mass deployment of police forces. The events were also called the "BlackBerry riots" since the rioters used mobile devices and social media to organize. As the riots spread to other cities and towns across the UK, the country witnessed a relatively new phenomenon spreading anti-social behavior in cascade-dynamics based on copy-and-paste violence.

In the aftermath political, social and academic figures fiercely debated the cause and context of the Blackberry riots. Attributions for the rioters' behavior included structural factors such as racism and economic decline, as well as cultural factors like crime, hooliganism, the breakdown of social morality, and gang culture. Connecting all these factors was the fact that the riots were rooted in several of London's neighborhoods sometimes referred to as *ghettos:* Tottenham Hale, Hackney, Brixton, Chingford, Walthamstow, Peckham, Enfield, Battersea, Croydon, Ealing, and East Ham. The landscape of the city itself played a structural role in the riots. But if social ghettos themselves are part of the problem by sustaining social change, how can one avoid them arising?

9.2.2 The Nature of Parallel Societies

The word *ghetto* originates from the Italian *getto*, meaning "foundry" (likely because the first ghetto was established in 1516 on the site of a foundry in Venice), or from the Italian *borghetto*, diminutive of *borgo* "borough". Nowadays the word is used to refer to districts where *one or several ethnic or social groups dominate, and where the separation from the rest of society is caused and reproduced by social and economic circumstances.*

In many minds a ghetto arises because humans prefer to be in the company of those whom resemble themselves the most. Or, put a bit differently pertaining to abortive integration: Because people from particular cultural spheres wish to isolate themselves from the surrounding society and create parallel societies. The simple idea is thus that the underlying cause of ghettoization must be found in a general preference for living in areas where the majority of people resemble oneself and where one's cultural norms rule. So naturally, when there is a free choice to settle wherever one is inclined (and can't otherwise afford), ghettos and ultimately parallel societies arise.

But parallel societies are obviously not desirable to the process of integration and the cohesion of democratic society and a good life in the city. In extension to the echo-chambers they cause, it's plain that mono-cultural enclaves easily lead to polarization and positions of extremism. But it takes two to tango. Very few who live in the London ghetto of Hackney would say no to a residence in the affluent Royal Borough of Kensington and Chelsea. Yet the problem is that there isn't any room for them there to let. And when "ethnic schools" emerge with a dominant number of immigrants in one part of town, it's only because of the simultaneous emergence of "white schools" in another part. If one insists on a simple truth saying that humans would rather be in the company of those who resemble themselves the most, the responsibility for the ghettoization of society therefore appears at least to be mutual. If this is true we seem to be caught somewhat in a deadlock.

But is it really true that the cause of ghettoization must necessarily be located in the fact that ethnic minorities and social groups always have a preference for maintaining the accustomed social conventions by settling in the vicinity of each

Fig. 9.1 Chessboard and the
segregation model

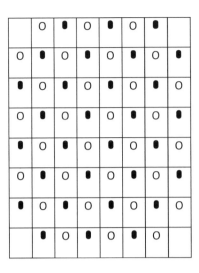

other? Of course, if that is truly the case, and if 'free choice' accordingly decides where one wants to settle, ghettoization is naturally the unavoidable final destination. If ghettoization additionally entails belief polarization, which then again leads to these ghettos ending up as cultural extremes (for example inordinate conservatism as is the case in both Hackney and Chelsea), the gap obviously becomes even wider. So when we observe that most people don't settle in an area where their neighbors don't resemble them much, isn't that evidence of the simple explanation being the correct one?

According to the economist Thomas Schelling there is a different and more complex possible explanation to ghettoization. It's an explanation, which provides some novel premises for understanding how the sweeping ghettoization of society occurs and what may be done to avoid the compartmentalization of cities.

In the late 1960s Schelling was sitting on a plane wondering how ghettos emerge. He especially contemplated whether it could really be true that ghettos arise because people don't wish to live in the vicinity of others who don't resemble and act like themselves. Schelling wondered whether ghettoization, "ethnic schools" and similar phenomena are logical consequences of intolerant attitudes and perhaps downright nationalism, culturalism or utter racism. Schelling constructed the surprising answer on a napkin, where after a little scribbling he reached an insight that was later verified with the help of his son's chessboard before it went around the world's lecture halls and computer simulations (Schelling 1978).

In the simple version of Schelling's chessboard- or, as it is now better known, *segregation model*, you take the chessboard out as well as a good handful of white and black Nine Men's Morris pieces. You fill the squares of the chessboard with alternately one white and one black piece for each square excepting the four corner squares (Fig. 9.1).

Now assume the chessboard is a model of a city, where each piece is a citizen or family household and each square is a residence. Each residence is surrounded by a number of 'neighbors' in the shape of the surrounding neighboring squares (8 for

Fig. 9.2 Segregation model
and Schelling's
randomization procedure

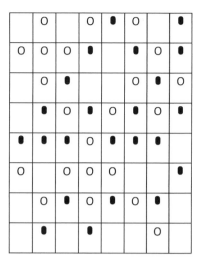

the most part, 5 for those along the edge of the board). Furthermore it's assumed that each piece has a 'moderate' or 'tolerant' attitude or preference with respect to the neighboring pieces. Hence each piece 'prefers' that just slightly more than one third of their neighbors are of the same color as the piece itself. Since the number of neighbors a resident can have is between 1 and 8, it's more precisely assumed that a resident is only content under the following circumstances:

- If he has only one neighbor, then she is the same color as him;
- If he has two neighbors, then at least one of them is the same color as him;
- If he has three, four or five neighbors, then at least two are the same color as him.
- If he has six, seven or eight, then at least three are the same color as him.

Such general preferences are called "moderate" in the sense that they appear to be anything but intolerant. After all, the residents seem satisfied and content even when a majority of their neighbors has another "color". Given this general preference it would seem quite misleading to describe the residents as falling under the simple assumption that they are unwilling to integrate with those who don't resemble themselves, not to say to describe them as being intolerant.

Now if you pay closer attention to the chessboard, the first thing you will notice is that the city in Fig. 9.1 isn't simply organized in a neat pattern. It is also one big mixed neighborhood or city, where everyone is satisfied with living in their square. But what if the allocation of residents isn't as well laid out to begin with?

To mix things up a bit, we follow Schelling's original procedure. We begin by removing 20 random pieces. We then choose five random empty squares, where a black or white piece is inserted with 50 % likelihood—a pretty random procedure. Following this random procedure the chessboard may end up in an array of different configurations. Figure 9.2 will serve as the example. Even though the residents are assumed to be just as tolerant as before, i.e. their preferences are unchanged, there are now 9 residents or families (six white and three black), who are no longer content

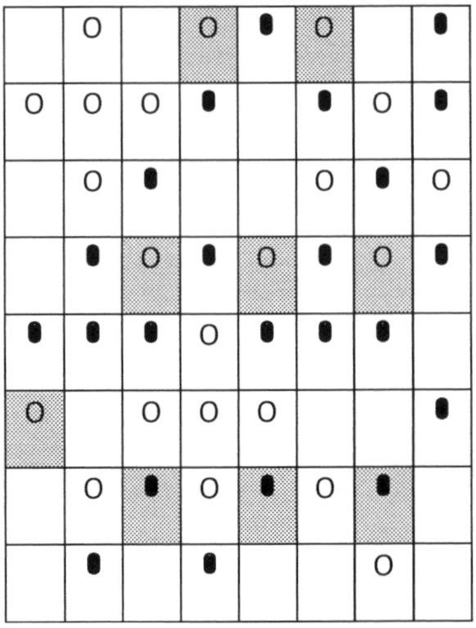

Fig. 9.3 Segregation model
and neighorhoods

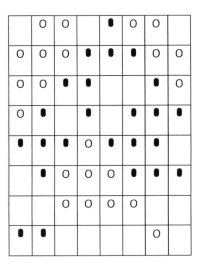

Fig. 9.4 One possible
outcome of segregation

with their residence due to their neighborhood. These are the marked cells in Fig. 9.3. The remaining 36 are content and live happily (in so far as Nine Men Morris pieces can live happily). Also, we're still looking at a mixed urban area, where even the unsatisfied residents have neighbors who resemble themselves.

Schelling's experiment now consists in moving, one by one, pieces that are discontent to an empty square, where they will become content. However, a consequence of this process is that the composition of residents changes in the area of the chessboard that the piece moves to as well as the neighborhood it left behind. Thereby new pieces may become discontent and may want to move. Schelling's surprising insight was, as illustrated in Fig. 9.4 and 9.5, that iterating this process ultimately and unavoidably leads the configuration of residents gradually but surely to segregate into separate groups, i.e. *ghettoization*.

Fig. 9.5 Another possible outcome of segregation

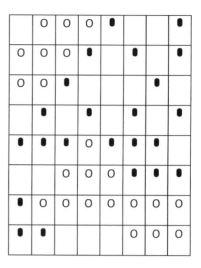

Figure 9.4 and 9.5 compose two of the possible end states that the original residence area from Fig. 9.2 can end up in. Both figures show segregation.

What's surprising about Schelling's segregation model is that with these assumptions it may demonstrated how ghettoization can occur, even when people have a moderate or tolerant attitude regarding whom they are surrounded by. It shows how it would be a mistake to infer intolerant attitudes from the macro-phenomenon of ghettoization. Computer simulations have since then shown that the model is exceptionally robust under a great variety of circumstances. Even with very high levels of tolerance and with very different allocations of residents, the model always ends up with a sweeping ghettoization or segregation of the groups.

The result of Schelling's segregation model is highly disconcerting. Even before one incorporates varying housing prices and income differences ghettoization appears to be the unavoidable end result. In contrast to the simple intuition we began with, one doesn't need to assume that ghettoization is due to a special social interest within social groups to huddle together. If observing general preferences that less than the majority of one's neighbors should be different from oneself, such an interest may just as well be the *consequence* of tensions which occur when socio-economic inequality, ghettoization and fear of others have taken hold, rather than the original *cause* of ghettoization—and one shouldn't mix cause and effect.

It's equally worrying that the areas of social life to which Schelling's model apply are not limited to how people choose to settle. The same process is also in play when it comes to other relevant decisions in society such as, for instance, job recruitment and the choice of which school to put your kids in.

In Europe, for instance, the share of immigrants in public schools has in recent years become a hot potato. Though few will admit to it, when parents consider what characterizes a good school this issue definitely factors into the decision. But even though the choice of school is in some places and countries the object of certain regulations, at least with respect to public schools, whereby ghettoization in part can be counteracted, the attractive liberalization of school choice prevalent in most countries causes a surrender of the school's student composition to the ruling socio-economic powers. Due to the increasing framing of the choice of school as partly dependent on the share of ethnic students, the result has been the unavoidable one, whether anyone wanted it or not. Even with extremely wide preferences pertaining to the share of immigrants or ethnic Europeans in one's child's class, many countries struggle helplessly with the ghettoization of public schools.

Of course, segregation may also work on several dimensions at the same time. Recently, school systems in the developed world have experienced a surge in parents insisting that their children are somehow "extra-ordinarily competent" and need special talent schools. But while these parents still only constitute a minority, Schelling's segregation model tells us that they will be able to start a chain-reaction that leads to the further ghettoization of schools into those for 'smart' students and those for the rest of us. Schelling's model also implies that solving such problems cannot be accomplished by reducing the collective problems facing our fundamental institutions to individual problems through the application of unwarranted simplicity based on uncertain inferences of individual motives from macro-phenomena. That would be too simple a model.

9.3 Why Democracy Is Not Just 'One Vote'

It's not only institutions of blood donation, cities and public schools, which have been objects of simplification in recent years. The conception of democracy itself appears to have changed significantly in this direction as well. Where politics during the 1970s and 1980s revolved around values and visions of the good life and the just society, today many view politics as a mere power struggle. In particular, it seems to have become more and more legitimate to vote purely based on one's own self-interests—recall the discussion of consumer democracy in Chap. 4. The act of casting one's vote is now roughly comparable to choosing the item one personally prefers on the shelf in the shopping aisle, no matter what other people may prefer, or what the consequences will be for them. After all, won't the political 'market forces' just aggregate these preferences to everyone's benefit? One individual, one vote—that's simple. What else could democracy mean?

However, if one transfers the insights from the institution of blood donation and ghettoization of cities respectively, to the growing conception of democracy as a consumer democracy, some interesting points emerge. The first point is that, as was the case with blood donation, polling in a democratic election ultimately constitutes a collective action problem. Viewed in isolation, we may all principally prefer that all citizens vote during a parliamentary election, rather than nobody voting. It's not much of a democracy without citizens in the ballot boxes. But, as long as it is just a representative segment of all citizens' votes, one's own vote doesn't really make any difference. The vote is absorbed in the statistics without moving mandates. Thus, if you expect that the share of citizens who venture to the ballot box is somewhere between a representative segment and *everyone*, then there is really no point in going down to the voting station and wasting your precious time putting a useless X on a worthless piece of paper.

Yet in democratic countries throughout the world, citizens line up to cast their votes. Does this mean that the citizens in democratic countries are extraordinarily irrational? Hardly. Recall that giving blood usually isn't an individual action based on simple cost-benefit analysis. Just as people give blood to qualify as responsible fellow citizens, people cast their vote to act as responsible citizens. Voting is part of a democratic identity, whether or not it changes anything.

Does this translate into saying, as often claimed by election reporters, that we may deduce from a macro-phenomenon of high turnout that democracy is healthy and well? As for inferring from ghettoization to individual motives, this is 'unfortunately' not the case. While ghettoization is possible without intolerance, so is voting without involvement; but while blood quality is principally independent of the blood donor's intentions, the quality of a democratic vote isn't. If it doesn't require anything else to qualify as a responsible citizen than voting, there is no incentive for each citizen to go any further into the political issues they vote upon. You can just vote according to your interest and still have a clear conscience without having gotten any further into what you are actually voting on. It is actually possible that the quality of the democratic election and hence the purpose of democracy could be better served by more people staying at home on the couch. Alternatively, just as people require transparency in politics, people could require quality in elections. This is obviously a controversial thing to say, if not downright "anti-democratic". Nevertheless it's true, inasmuch as one believes that a precondition of democracy isn't just that people vote, but also have relevant information about *what they are voting about or upon*. It's perhaps also the root of an explanation for why politics to an increasing extent seems to be more and more about interest groups, special issues and personal taxation, than about politics.

Low quality democracy is however not the only consequence of the too simple ideas behind the consumer democracy's scourge. What characterizes consumer democracy is not just the increasing legitimacy to vote on the basis of one's own special interests, whether it's about economy, environmental- or national politics. It is also a particular indifference and ignorance with respect to the complex health of democratic institutions—that is, with respect to the details of how these institutions aggregate political opinions fairly. To see why this is dangerous we have to go shopping for toys.

Every Friday Pelle takes his son to a toy-store, where the kid gets to choose *one* toy. Now this thought might shock parents who know how difficult it is for children to handle complex decision problems that stretch over so many shelves of toys. Pelle's solution is however to let his son take those things down from the shelves that he finds interesting—say, 3 toys.

Next, the 3 toys are placed on the floor, where the boy is presented with the toys in pairs of two and asked which of the two he prefers. This is repeated for all 3 possible pairs (A, B), (B, C), (A, C). The preferences (>) could for instance be these:

$$A > B$$
$$B > C$$
$$A > C$$

The ability to choose which of the two possibilities in a pair one prefers (or is indifferent between) is called *completeness* of preferences. It's a so-called *rationality axiom*—one of the fundamental rules our preferences over possible consequences of our actions must respect to qualify as rational. Another rationality axiom is that of *transitivity*. Transitivity means that if you prefer A to B, and B to C, then you also prefer A to C . . . if you are rational at any rate. Pelle now assumes transitivity for his son, and since he picks A to B in the first round, and B to C in the second, Pelle puts toy C back on the shelf. Finally, his son is presented once again with the choice between A and B, just to confirm the original preference for A, after which toy A is bought.

Both the completeness axiom and the transitivity axiom are bordering between the 'normative' and the 'descriptive'. On the one hand they dictate what is rational (how one *ought* to choose to qualify as being rational). On the other hand they also describe some fundamental norms for what people demand of each other to call one another's choices rational. For instance imagine a couple on a dinner date who are presented with a menu with three different courses. Here it would probably cause one party a bit of concern if the other party insisted that he couldn't make a choice, because he couldn't compare each dish to the others; or, maybe even worse, if he prefers A to B and B to C, but C to A! With such a person at the table, it can quickly turn into a very long evening. Nonetheless Pelle doesn't have any problems with the method when it comes to getting his son to pick a toy, and that is for one thing because he performs the operations step by step to uncover complete and transitive preferences, which are necessary to refer to the boy's choice as rational, and rightly so. In this way the axioms are also descriptive—at least when it comes to a simple individual decision problem such as choosing what toy to acquire.

Could these axioms also be transferred to collective decisions, such as elections? It would be great if you could simply aggregate all of society's individuals' preferences in this way—the way of consumer democracy—and have that political elections would then be characterized as rational. That way we could by each voting according to our individual preferences simultaneously ensure that the outcome of the elections would also be in our common interest.

That's in any case what Pelle convinced Vincent and their mutual student Rasmus of in connection with their monthly lunch . . . as Pelle told them: "What could be a better procedure than precisely the one mentioned above, which adheres to completeness, transitivity and the rest of the pool of rationality axioms?" However, it was in this way that he alone got to decide on the restaurant every time they went to lunch, and it was also how Rasmus and Vincent learned how the way the voting procedure is wired means almost everything when one votes based on one's special interest without paying attention to the procedure for aggregating preferences.

In order to understand why Pelle could end up always having his way despite a democratic vote, a piece of background information is required. It is common knowledge to the three friends that Rasmus who is a student has the least money, while Vincent who is a professor earns the most. Pelle, who is in the spring of his career, falls somewhere in-between. This means that whenever the three friends are going out to lunch, Rasmus usually prefers student-houses in the lower range, Vincent prefers restaurants that are slightly more expensive and Pelle opts for cafés in between.

Now take the choice procedure Pelle used to help his son pick a toy, and apply it to the three friends' common decision problem. Thus, each of the three friends first gets to name the place they would like to go for lunch. That gives three possibilities: *A, B* and *C*. Next, the three alternatives are paired in every possible way: *(A, B), (B, C), (A, C)*. Finally, for each pair there is a vote about which of the two possibilities in the pair each of the three friends would prefer to dine at.

It is now obvious why Pelle always ends up getting his way. As long as each always votes on the place to eat in the selected pair, which is price-wise closest to his favourite place, and that the three places respectively have, say, the following prices for lunch,

$$A = \$5, \qquad B = \$10, \qquad C = \$15$$

the vote always results in Pelle's preferred café (B) being chosen.

To see why, first observe that the voting procedure determining what place to go eat results in a series of pair-wise disjoint choices as relevant: *(A, B), (B, C)*, and *(A, C)*. Each member of the lunch group then votes for the place that is closest to his preferred price range. This means that each vote on which place to eat results in the following scenarios, where the place that receives most votes is subsequently chosen:

- First *A* is compared to *B*, which leads to two votes for *B* and one for *A*. Hence it can be deduced that $B > A$.
- Then one compares *A* to *C*, which (when Pelle for the sake of appearances declares his solidarity with the poor student) gives two votes for *A* and one for *C*, i.e. $A > C$.
- Due to transitivity it now follows that $B > C$, which is also confirmed by a possible vote, where *B* receives two votes and *C* only one.

Consequently we can say that $B > A > C$. For these preferences the rationality axioms have been satisfied, and *B* is chosen. Note that this is always the case as long as Pelle's preferred price lies between Rasmus' and Vincent's. In this case Pelle is called a *median voter*, because there are precisely as many people who prefer a pricier place to eat than Pelle, as there are people who prefer a cheaper place to eat than him (a single one on each side). Besides the fact that the median voter is always on the winning side in a vote like this, it's also always Pelle's preferred suggestion that is chosen.

In one sense the result is positively based on our normative standards. It's a case of democratic voting, and the result satisfies the rationality axioms. In another sense the result is a negative one. In spite of Pelle only constituting a third of the voting body, he gets his way every time, while Rasmus and Vincent must always accept a political compromise. Now, one could naturally maintain that the result is democratic, since Pelle represents the 'sensible', economic golden mean. That would however be ignoring the fact that a system where one takes turns in choosing a place to eat would end up with the same economic result $(5 + 10 + 15)/3$, as if Pelle's café is chosen every time: 10 USD.

The point of this example isn't only to explain why so-called center parties have extraordinary power when there is a vote in the parliamentary chamber, or that Vincent and Rasmus could repress Pelle by forming an alliance voting on shifts for A and C. Rather, the point is that the decision frame for a democratic election, which combines a political continuum with the notion of voting in accordance with individual special interests, can have a line of tangible and detrimental consequences. In the example above, the relevant choice has already passed once Pelle's voting procedure has been enacted, and each person votes in his own individual interest without thinking of the bigger picture. The politically relevant choice for real is which procedure should be used as the actual decision frame for the democratic election. Imagine thus, that Rasmus and Vincent had predicted the consequences of Pelle's suggestion of decision frame, i.e. the choice procedure, and had subsequently suggested that one must first choose between this and then a rotation round. It would mean that the decisive vote would no longer be about which café each individual preferred regardless of the others' preferences, but between a voting procedure based on special interests and a voting procedure which takes the greater relation between everyone's special interest into account. It would be rational here for Rasmus and Vincent to vote for the rotation system, while Pelle would be the sole voter for a system based on special interests.

9.4   Comparing Society to Company

The point of discussing voting procedures is much the same as in the discussion related to blood banks and the growing ghettoization of society. What are the consequences if we apply too simplistic models—such as consumer democracy—to our collective institutions? What are the dangers if we forget to frame our institutions in larger perspectives and more extensive visions of a good and fair society, in favour of too simplistic ideas about the nature, effects and value of immediate choices that are focused on individual's interests? Our guess is that we will end up undermining our very own interests, by undermining the common institutions that are supposed to secure them in the long run.

Believing that all motives are compatible with economic incentives may undermine invaluable charity institutions that provide goods to all of us for which we do not pay. Making unwarranted inferences about the micro-motives underlying macro-phenomena such as ghettoization may lead us to ignore as well as devise the wrong solutions to the nature and dynamics of some of the biggest and most complex institutions that human beings have ever created. Embracing consumer democracy may put us on a road where democracy is either about those who have a majority and singlehandedly rule over those who are in a minority (although it will never be democratic that 51 % of a population let their special interests decide over the remaining 49 %), or have the smarter outsmart the rest of us to believe that as long as we get a say amongst predefined options, we're also the ones in charge. Common to all such simplifications is the failure to realize that true democracy presupposes that complex collective problems are treated as such, not simplified too much.

Chapter 10
Democracy in Control

*If knowledge can create problems, it is not through ignorance
that we can solve them.*

—Isaac Asimov

Throughout *Infostorms* a stockpile of examples has been compiled to show how information may be used to enlighten and inform individuals and groups from all walks of life. Unfortunately, an equal, if not larger, stock of cases has been advanced showing how information may be used to manipulate people, opinions and markets and derail individual as well as collective reason and rationality.

The infostorm is like any other storm. It does not cast sidelong glances at the scenery over which it sweeps. The ignorance, cascades, bystanders, bubbles, framing- and polarization effects may ravage everywhere. The storm depends largely on the quantity and/or quality of the information available to the decision-maker, then coupled with some sort of social proof and finally accelerated to the speed of light by modern information technology.

Pluralistic ignorance, lack of sufficient information and social proof were at work in Computer City while deliberating over the purchase of a new laptop; information in abundance and more reliance on social proof gave rise to informational cascades confusing us about which airport terminal to go to in order to catch the flight from New York JFK to Paris Charles de Gaule; cascades appear in bubbles and band-wagons in science trends, management and funding; framing effects and cleverly designed presentations of information penetrated everything from insurance policies to potential measures against deadly diseases, war efforts and troop deployments, blood donation, where to go for lunch and consumer democracy; polarization as a result of information selection and one-sided information osmosis was responsible for teenage mocking on social media, attacks on the euro currency generated by unsubstantiated rumours on a blog, partisan politics in the US. . . . The list goes on and on.

Not catching a plane is one thing, bubbles on opinion and financial markets that shake things up severely is yet another. "Likes" and other upvote derivatives may appear as innocent and unreflective gestures on social media, but can be used to foster murderous cyber-bullying that only halts at "todding". Co-existence among humans is one big complex exercise of respect for the individual and collective coordination. Democratic co-existence is equally mosaic. Everyone having a vote does not characterize a robust democracy, but everyone having an *informed* vote does. For smooth-running democracies, information is at the forefront for individuals as

V. F. Hendricks, P. G. Hansen, *Infostorms*, DOI 10.1007/978-3-319-03832-2_10,
© Springer International Publishing Switzerland 2014

well as groups. And given the potential infostorms, modern democracies may become hard to maintain and develop.

Deliberation, decision, choice and action all require information; not only when you need to make up your mind as to which new computer to buy or insurance policy to choose. No, generally and far more importantly, whenever citizens navigate in democracy, information is required. Not any information will do; *correct* information, properly formatted and handled is required, since what may appear as a robust modern democracy is acutely sensitive to junk-evidence spreading and infostorms blowing.

10.1   Yesterday's Democracy

Humans are the only species on this planet who have chosen to configure and live in a democracy—no other species on Earth do that to our knowledge. From a historical perspective democracy is a rather recent addition to the human repository of ideas. Homo sapiens as a species is approximately 200,000 years old. The behavioural characteristics that man is known by today only date back about 50,000 years. The earliest documented notions of democratic thinking may yet only be traced back to the Athenian democracy of ancient Greece around 400–500 years BCE.

The word democracy is derived from the Greek *demos*, which means "people" and *kratos* meaning "power". The philosopher, who in Antiquity systematically treated the term for the first time, was Plato—and he was not a big fan of democracy as a way of government. Rather than a monarchy with one ruler, or a timocracy consisting of a ruling class of landowners, Plato above all preferred some sort of oligarchy, where the ruling power is made up of a narrow elitist class. Plato would have liked to see this ruling elitist class consisting of ... indeed philosophers, called "philosopher kings", who would be the guardians of his utopian Callipolis. There was method to this apparent madness, insofar as the most enlightened and truth-seeking individuals were, according to Plato, the philosophers, and in this way it became a self-fulfilling megalomaniac prophecy that they were to rule.

Democracy had, according to Plato, the deficiency that truth cannot be decided by majority rule. Plato would, in all likelihood, have stuck to his guns even had he been presented with Condorcet's jury theorem about 2000 years down the road (Chap. 6). Condorcet's jury theorem is from the time of the Enlightenment, when modern democratic thoughts, principles, guidelines and procedures were earnestly formulated. But once again, in light of human history spanning 200,000 years, it almost seems like yesterday that we developed the nifty idea of democracy. Thus mankind's horizon of experience with this form of government is strictly speaking rather limited, while we have many—and at times rather questionable—experiences with monarchies, oligarchies, timocracies and other "top-down" forms of ruling.

Common to all kinds of government, if they are to work in any sort of reasonable way, is the need of information. There must be someone (one, some or all) sufficiently enlightened, with enough sense and sensibility, to, on a suitably informed basis, deliberate, decide, choose and act for one, some or all. One may then debate whether this should be a monarch, a cluster of hedge funds, private landowners, multinational pharmaceutical companies or large IT-corporations as a timocracy would probably look like nowadays, or whether this skill set of edification and reason should be delegated to the individual citizen in a common democracy.

Plato would agree with this information requirement as it fits ruling. He would agree with even more. Information as beliefs about one thing or the other isn't enough to rule with, since beliefs don't have to be true. Many of us may after all believe, or be convinced, that Albert Einstein was awarded the Nobel Prize in Physics for his theory of relativity. It's true that we believe accordingly, but it's not true that Einstein got the Nobel Prize for relativity theory. He received it for his theory of photoelectric effect, and that is something completely different. Believing doesn't make it so. Beliefs don't have to be true, nor does information, as this book bears witness to. Neither beliefs nor information automatically have veracity attached to them; one may be informed of something false, just as one may be convinced of something, which turns out to be false. Epistemology needs a third way—and so does democracy. It is time for *knowledge* democracy as opposed to the consumer or post-factual ditto.

10.2   Post-Factual Democracy

The information age may possibly be responsible for fostering a new beast: The post-factual democracy where facts are replaced by opportune narratives, where the good story is a viral one, and where politics is simply about maximizing voter support. The American presidential election of 2012 presented some striking examples of the new beast rearing its head.

On August 29, 2012, the Republican candidate for the vice presidency, Paul Ryan, made a speech which Fox News characterized by three words "dazzling, deceiving, distracting" and referred to as "an apparent attempt to set the world record for the greatest number of blatant lies and misrepresentations slipped into a single political speech. On this measure, while it was Romney who ran the Olympics, Ryan earned the gold".[1] By way of example, Ryan tried to blame the Obama administration for the downgrading of the US credit rating, but the fact of the matter is that the credit rating was diminished because the Republicans threatened not to raise the debt ceiling. Ryan likewise tried to pin the closing of a General Motors factory plant in Janesville, Wisconsin on President Obama while the plant was actually shut down under President George W. Bush. One should not forget that Ryan had earlier on asked for federal funds to save the factory while Republican presidential nominee Mitt Romney consistently criticized the Obama administration for setting the auto industry bailout plan in motion.

---

[1] Kohn, S. (2012). "Paul Ryan's speech in three words", *FoxNews.com*, August 30.

Romney himself later jumped the post-factual bandwagon at a rally in Defiance, Ohio by trying to establish a narrative about Chrysler's plans to move the entire production of the Jeep to China. The truth of the matter is that Chrysler had plans to make Jeeps in China but not to sell back to the US market and certainly no plans to shut down the production lines in Michigan, Illinois and Ohio.[2]

During the election, the Democrats also tried moves that were perpendicular to the narrow track of truth. On the question of whether Romney had offshore accounts hiding money in tax havens, Democrat election teams produced a video in which they had asked random people the simple question whether they had offshore bank accounts. Naturally, the ones who answered said "No!" The video went on YouTube and the Obama campaign referred to stories in Associated Press and *Vanity Fair* about overseas bank accounts followed by the text: "Is he (Romney) avoiding paying US taxes by having money in those tax havens?" and "Was he trying to hedge against the dollar by having a Swiss bank account".[3]

There are quite a few narratives like this out there and they can be very advantageous for a certain political agenda if they can be made to stick and become robust. The Internet is an excellent medium for padding stories through "likes", upvotes, comments, reads, threads and views, which over a relatively short period may cause the narrative to go viral. But what is viral is not necessarily true, and what is true is not necessarily viral. Maximizing votes does not require facts no matter how much we would like it to be so, but then again voter maximization does not add up to democracy. If democracy doesn't have access to reliable sources of information and doesn't respect valid argument, then there is no way of distinguishing between junk evidence and facts. Without the ability to make this distinction we may be welcoming the post-factual democracy. It is neither democratic nor a function of the US geography—it is worldwide.

10.3   The Democracy of Truth

Plato defined knowledge in his dialogues *Meno* and *Theaetetus*. He needed it as much for his oligarchy as we need it today for a modern democracy. The classic definition, still largely prevalent, considers knowledge to be true justified belief. Person a knows A, if and only if (1) a believes A, (2) A is true, and (3) a is justified in believing A.

Person a believing proposition A merely means that a must be somehow cognitively connected to the proposition which ultimately is to be known. This cognitive connection may be called believing. Beliefs may be understood as a kind of psychological primitive, or if one prefers, we as humans are disposed to form and have beliefs. Condition (1) simply connects the person to the proposition, which in the end is the object of knowledge. Condition (2) is far more interesting, since according

---

[2] Miller, J. (2012). "Romney cites incorrect auto manufacturing claim in Ohio", *CBS News*, October 26.

[3] Jackson, D. (2012). "Obama video hits Romney on offshore accounts", *USA Today*, July 5.

to the standard definition *a* can't, if the subject *knows A*, know something false. That would not be knowledge, even though it is quite conceivable that you believe, think, hope, expect, feel or for that matter, are informed of *A*. Knowledge cannot be defined without paying attention to the facts. Facts are manifestations of truth, and truth is yet again a necessary, but not sufficient condition for knowledge. This feature applies to the philosophical definition of knowledge, but it also applies if one is to rule based on democratic principle. Such ruling requires facts and truth.

Preferring democracy as the best way to configure and rule a state is basically a position, a belief or a viewpoint but it doesn't make everything that takes place in a democracy a stance, belief or subjective point of view. From any form of government there follow a number of facts. A sovereign regent characterizes a monarchy. If the regent is defied, the robustness of the government form is defied. To question or doubt the tyrant often carries unfortunate consequences such as decapitation in days of old, or other ways of being removed from the scene for shorter or longer periods of time.

From a democracy, a collection of facts similarly follow concerning everything from the tripartition of power and the parliament of representatives, to a market- or centrally planned economy and so forth. A number of institutions are installed to safeguard, regulate and take part in optimizing the democratic structure that one has attitudinally been able to agree on.

More specifically a line of institutions is installed that amount to democratic indicators and guardians. Public officials who investigate citizens' complaints against the government come to mind, along with various other investigative committees, national auditors and so forth. Their job generally consists in uncovering, collecting, analysing and assessing the facts or consequences which the democratic form of government occasions—from legal complaints to accusations of fraud, corruption etc. These institutions have to meet stringent criteria of impartiality and often even scientific probity precisely to ensure that what follows from the chosen form of government isn't just something one can doubt at random, disregard or archive in the waste-bin as advertisements for various political products. Among politicians there is a widespread tendency to appoint fact-finding commissions, investigative committees and so on. The mandate of these commissions and committees is to produce and summarize knowledge and evidence as the basis for political deliberation, decision and action. Often enough, at the same rate that these commissions have delivered their findings politicians have routinely questioned the results brought forth: Especially when they haven't proven advantageous for a certain political agenda.

Whilst in a monarchy one may risk life and limb in questioning the legitimacy of the regent, one doesn't receive capital punishment in a democracy for questioning those institutions which safeguard, regulate and develop the fundamental structure of society. Luckily one can make objections both of a political nature and regarding the quality of the facts the democratic institutions may base their actions upon. The latter however requires that one can produce better results or facts. By contrast, it's completely free of charge and contrary to the democratic form of government to comfortably claim that those institutions which clarify un₁ opular facts are merely political agents or plainly mistaken in spite of their composition and intended impartiality. Roughly speaking, if we waive the respect for facts and truth, we waive the respect for democracy. Facts and truth, or in short, *true information*, is a necessary, but not sufficient condition for knowledge, and also for democracy.

In his recent book, Fukuyama (2012) points to the fact that corruption is a lurking danger in every government body because of the human inclination to favour him/herself, family and friends. In the fight against corruption, the establishment of trust and the construction of communal institutions is the first law of building a state. A fundamental premise is to understand how democracy works as social interaction and coordination. The coordination game is often played by having a pretty good idea of the strategies of other players in order to either act in concert with or block them in order to maximize personal utility—or by realizing that the greatest payoff for everybody is realized by cooperation and coordination. The latter is the lesson from the Prisoner's dilemma: Every citizen realizes that the aim of maximizing personal utility may facilitate forms of government which are democratically questionable and often lead to the oppression of other individuals and groups. That goes for everybody below the top of the oligarchy or regent. Such a position is naturally reserved for the select few, which may explain why democracy is to be preferred over and above the other rules of government. By cooperation and coordination, the utility will be greater for all.

There is a price to pay. Everybody must give up the same amount of sovereignty to the societal institutions. In return, the managers of power are obligated to carefully and correctly respect the common rules set forth. Democracy is really the answer to a challenging coordination problem. The ability to institutionalize norms of trust, objectivity and impartiality are the beacons of democracy. Without these beacons democratic coordination is impossible. Thus when players, especially those who define the rules of the game such as government heads, spin doctors and public officials begin perfunctory practice with the truth and exercise corruption then that would be like letting a lion loose among the zebras. Abuse of power may lead to systemic distrust, which in turn may spread like a cascade through the societal system.

10.4 Process Democracy

The classic definition of knowledge contains a third condition pertaining to the relationship between a person's beliefs and their truth. If the only two conditions for knowledge are that you have beliefs and they are true, nothing stands in the way of you getting such true beliefs by way of revelations, lucky guesswork or plain coincidence.

Knowledge meanwhile isn't wired like that. The third condition is installed to ensure that one may always be called to account for one's knowledge with an argument or some other justifying structure explaining why conditions (1) and (2) (person *a* believes *A*, and *A* is true) are appropriately connected. So to refer to your 'gut feeling' is not good enough when you have to argue for actually having true assumptions. 'Gut feelings', crystal balls, mystical insights or subtle hunches are not considered *reliable procedures, processes or methods* through which true beliefs are acquired.

A substantial share of contemporary epistemology is about uncovering the cognitive processes considered reliable procedures (or truth-tracking processes) for acquiring true beliefs. Knowledge is, crudely speaking, true information acquired by a reliable method of inquiry (Hendricks 2006).

This understanding of knowledge is directly transferable to the democracy theme. Deliberations, decisions, choices and actions performed by agents individually or collectively in various settings, including central democratic ones like voting, are extraordinarily sensitive to how the available information is processed. Pluralistic ignorance, information cascades, framing effects, polarization, echo-chambers, bias and bandwagons, bystanders, bubbles, and bad belief aggregations are all examples of the available information being incorrectly processed, either because there is too little or too much information, or the information is presented, sorted, selected and shared in a way where social proof is not conducive to truth. If the information is incorrectly processed there is no guaranteeing its truthfulness, and if there is no guarantee of its truthfulness, then there is a free passage for manipulating citizens, decision makers and other agents in a democracy.

10.5   Control Problems

From a macro-perspective, democracy may thus be viewed as a kind of information structure with agents as nodes and information channels as vertices. Some agents can send, other agents can receive, and some can send and receive messages to and from each other. Some information channels are open, others are closed, and some channels are re-routed around certain agents so they do not to gain access to certain information; some information is common knowledge, some is not and so forth. Some believers are true believers, some are deviants, some follow the herd guided by social proof, others have additional evidence leading them not to believe and so forth. And all this happens in the sandbox commonly referred to as 'society', which cherishes a recent notion called democracy. Running a democracy right becomes much like an *engineering control problem;* not controlling the production on an assembly line or the construction of a high-rise building project, but the control of information among interacting agents, a.k.a. citizens (Hansen et al. 2013).

From a micro-perspective the control problem analogy works too. For instance, bystander-effects may be turned into informational cascades and vice versa, as indicated in Chap. 2; pluralistic ignorance may be generated by the ways in which agents reason about the interpretation and decision rules of other agents; rules which, if changed, may be used to account for the dynamics of bystanders. Informational cascades and bandwagons also turn out to be similar as bandwagons roughly may be considered cascading phenomena with aggregated public signals but no private signals (Hendricks and Rendsvig 2014).

In general, the information phenomena under scrutiny here are *composites*—including agents, beliefs, public/private signals, preferences, expectations, interpretation and decision rules, network topology etc. The ambition of the philosophical or information-theoretic program tacitly outlined in this treatise is to uncover the common formal or logical structure of the above information-driven social phenomena and others like them studied in social psychology and behavioural and theoretical economics: Bandwagon effects, boom thinking, group thinking, herd behaviour, gullibility, conformity, compliance, bubbles etc. all somehow, and to some extent, rely on social proof. Then study the phenomena *modularly* such that every composite phenomenon may be tweaked as to agents, beliefs, signals, rules, expectations, network topology etc. The challenge then becomes how one may get from one phenomenon to the next by unplugging one module, tweaking another, replacing a third ... plug it all in, wired it up correctly, and press play to see if one arrives at the information phenomena under study.

It would indeed be odd if every socio-psychological information phenomenon was distinct and had nothing to do with the next; again, they do all rely on social proof. There is hardly one exclusive kind of reasoning capacity, or reasoning compartment, reserved for compliance and yet another disparate one reserved for conformity; they are related somehow and figuring out what this relation amounts to in terms of modularity is an information control problem.

10.6 Short Summary

The "information age" in which information, true as well as false, flows freely between agents is not necessarily good for democracy as an information structure. The information structure needs guidelines and procedures whereby information may be processed in such a way that it leads to truthful, appropriately formatted information, which may be used for correct decision, rational vigour and reason without clouds. The truth is always popular, even though it might be an imposition. Fraudulent dealings with wrongfully processed or formatted information are fraudulent dealings with knowledge, which then again is what democracy rests upon and should be ruled according to.

It all sounds nice and dandy philosophically, but it doesn't immediately provide instructions in practice. In this loosely formulated decision- and democracy-matter, what kind of tangible procedures or 'junior woodchuck codes' ensure that citizens acquire knowledge and won't drown while trying to take a sip from the fire hydrant of information?

As a matter of course numerous such procedures may be outlined. To give a short summary and hopefully prepare you for dodging and dealing with a number of information phenomena mentioned in *Infostorms:*

1. Never accept that your own or others' ignorance or lack of insight constitute a justifying argument for not gathering more information. If there's not enough information available, seek or ask for more, even if it may seem embarrassing to

want more truths. That's how you may avoid ending up in a state of pluralistic ignorance.

2. Do not without reflection assume views or do something just because everyone else assumes or does it, and by so doing simply imitate what others do or think. If you really think there's smoke in the kitchen, then it's probably because there is. Take notice of this and you may avoid falling for the bystander-effect.

3. Consider the source(s) of your information. Is it of such a nature that not only may you state that you believe it, but also why—and similarly why others should also accept its truthfulness? By doing so you may steer clear of many informational cascades, bandwagons, herds and lemmings.

4. Most decisions you are faced with are inevitably formulated in frames, where the choices are set up in such a way that favours one option over one or several others. Consider whether you agree with the favouritism the frame or perspective on the decision problem elicits. Such deliberations can be part of avoiding framing effects.

5. Agreement alone is not a sign of the truthfulness of the information converged on. In addition, agreement may be strengthened by deliberation, so if you incidentally agree with others, deliberation can plainly lead to a strengthened agreement and in worst-case, extremism. Tap information from those you agree with, tap information from those you disagree with, triangulate with independent sources, then deliberate on your own and see where that takes you. That may just lead you away from polarization and echo-chambers.

6. Be aware that the important choices concern the choice of decision-frame, and not the trivial daily choices concerning two litres of whole vs. skimmed milk.

References

Abbott, A. (2013). Brain-simulation and graphene projects win billion-euro competition. Nature Online. http://www.nature.com. Accessed 23 Jan 2013.

Ariely, D. (2009). *Predictably irrational: The hidden forces that shape our decisions.* London: HarperCollins.

Austin, J. (1975). *How to do things with words* (2nd ed.). Oxford: Oxford University Press.

Becker, R. B. (2004). Are markets inefficient? *Lecture notes for financial economics* (p. E425) Indiana: Indiana University.

Bikhchandani, S., Hirshleifer, D., & Welch, I. (1998). Learning from the behavior of others: Conformity, fads, and informational cascades. *Journal of Economic Perspectives, 12,* 151–170.

Black, F. (1985). Noise. *Journal of Finance, 41*(3), 529–543.

Boensvang, H., Hendricks, V. F., & Rendsvig, R. K. (2014). Beware Bystanders. forthcoming

Budtz Pedersen, D., Hansen, P. G., & Hendricks, V. F. (2012, Oct 20). Sandheden til salg for junk-evidens. *Politiken*, 8.

Budtz Pedersen, D., & Hendricks, V. F. (2013). Science bubbles. *Philosophy and Technology, 27*(3), 359–372.

Budtz Pedersen, D. (2013). Research Evaluation. *Ethics, Science, Technology, and Engineering.* Macmillan Reference (in press).

Buchanan, M. (2008, July 19). Why economic rheory is out of whack. *New Scientist.*

Button, K. S., Ioannidis, J. P. A., Mokrysz, C., Nosek, B. A., Flint, J., Robinson, E. S. J., & Munafò, M. R. (2013, April 10). Power failure: Why small sample size undermines the reliability of neuroscience. *Nature Reviews Neuroscience.*

Cialdini, R. (2007). *Influence: The psychology of persuasion.* Harper Collins Publishers.

Centola, D., Willer, R., & Macy, M. (2005). The Emperor's dilemma: A computational model of self-enforcing norms. *American Journal of Sociology, 110*(4), 1009–1040.

Chwe, M. S.-Y. (2001). *Rational ritual: Culture, coordination, and common knowledge.* Princeton University Press.

Cooper, J., Kelly, K. A., & Weaver, K. (2004). Attitudes, norms and social groups. In M. B. Brewer & M. Hewstone (Eds.), *Social cognition* (pp. 244–267). Oxford: Blackwell Publishing.

Cubitt, R., & Sugden, R. (2003, Oct). Common knowledge, salience, and convention: A reconstruction of David Lewis' game theory. *Economics and Philosophy, 19*(2), 175–210.

Darley, J. M., & Latané, B. (1969). Bystander 'apathy'. *American Scientist, 57,* 244–268.

Druckman, J. (2001a). Evaluating framing effects. *Journal of Economic Psychology, 22,* 96–101.

Druckman, J. (2001b). Using credible advice to overcome framing effects. *Journal of Law, Economics, and Organization, 17,* 62–82.

Entman, R. M. (1993). Framing: Toward clarification of a fractured paradigm. *Journal of Communication, 43,* 51–58.

Frank, R. (2000). *Luxur fever: Money and happiness in an era of excess.* Princeton: Princeton University Press.

Fukuyama, F. (2012). *The origins of political order*. New York: Farrar, Strauss and Giroux.

Gerrans, P. (2009, July 9). Bubble trouble. *Times Higher Education*.

Gilovich, T., Savitsky, K., & Medvec, V. H. (1998). The illusion of transparency: Biased assessments of others' ability to read one's emotional states. *Journal of Personality and Social Psychology, 75*(2), 332–346.

Gladwell, M. (2000). *The tipping point: How little things can make a big difference*. New York: Little, Brown and Company.

Gläser, J., & Whitley, R. (2007). The changing governance of the sciences. In R. Whitley (Ed.), *The advent of research evaluation systems* (pp. 3–27). Dordrecht: Springer.

Halbesleben, J. R. B., & Buckley, M. R. (2004). Pluralistic ignorance: Historical development and organizational applications. *Journal of Management History, 42*(1), 126–138.

Hansen, P. G., & Hendricks, V. F. (2007). Anerkendelsens økonomi og oplysningens værdi i det offentlige rum. *KRITIK*, #190, december, 41–51.

Hansen, P. G., & Hendricks, V. F. (2011). *Oplysningens blinde vinkler: En åndselitær kritik af informationssamfundet*. Copenhagen: Forlaget Samfundslitteratur.

Hansen, P. G., Hendricks, V. F., & Rendsvig, R. K. (2013, April). Infostorms. *Metaphilosophy, 44*(3), 301–326.

Hendricks, V. F. (2010, April). Knowledge transmissibility and pluralistic ignorance. *Metaphilosophy, 41*(3), 279–291.

Hendricks, V. F., & Rasmussen, J. L. (2012). *Nedtur! Finanskrisen forstået filosofisk*. Copenhagen: Gyldendal Business.

Hendricks, V. F., & Rendsvig, R. K. (2014a). *Modules and signals for BBC: Bystanders, Bandwagons and Cascades*, in preparation.

Hendricks, V. F., & Rendsvig, R. K. (Eds.). (2014b). *Socio-epistemic phenomena: 5 questions*. New York: Automatic Press/VIP.

Katz, D., & Allport, F. H. (1931). *Student attitudes*. Syracuse: Craftsman.

Krech, D., & Crutchfield, R. S. (1948). *Theories and problems of social psychology*. New York: McGraw-Hill.

Kroman, M. K. (2013). *Investeringer og holdninger*, report. Copenhagen: University of Copenhagen.

Kroman, M. K., & Hendricks, V. F. (2014). Opinion bubbles. forthcoming.

Laudel, G. (2006). The art of getting funded: How scientists adapt to their funding conditions. *Science and Public Policy, 33*(7), 489–504.

Layman, G. C., Carsey, T. M., Green, J. C., & Herrera, R. (2005). Party Polarization and "conflict extension" in the United States: he case of party activists. Presented at the *Annual Meeting of the South Political Science Association*. New Orleans.

Layman, G. C., Carsey, T. M., & Horowitz, J. M. (2006). Party polarization in American politics. *Annual Review of Political Science, 9*, 83–110.

Lee, I. H. (1998). Market crashes and informational avalanches. *Review of Economic Studies, 65*, 741–759.

List, C., & Goodin, R. E. (2001). Epistemic democracy: Generalizing the Condorcet Jury Theorem. *Journal of Political Philosophy, 9*, 277–306.

Lynch, M. P. (2010). Democracy as a Space of Reasons. In J. Elkins & A. Norris (Eds.), *Truth in Politics* (pp. 249–270). Philadelphia: University of Pennsylvania Press.

Mackie, D. M., & Cooper, J. (1984). Group polarization: The effects of group membership. *Journal of Personality and Social Psychology, 46*, 575–585.

Mallaby, S. (2010). *More money than god: Hedge funds and the making of a new elite*. Penguin Press.

Manning, R., Levine, M., & Collins, A. (2007). The Kitty Genovese murder and the social psychology of helping: The parable of the 38 witnesses. *American Psychologist, 62*(6), 555–562.

McCarty, N., Poole, K. T., & Rosenthal, H. (2013). *Political bubbles: Financial crises and the failure of American democracy*. Princeton: Princeton University Press.

Mellström, C., & Johannesson, M. (2008). Crowding out in blood donation: Was Titmuss right?. *Journal of the European Economic Association, 6*(4), 845–863. MIT Press.

Mirowski, P. (2013). The modern commercialization of science is a passel of Ponzi schemes. *Social Epistemology, 26*(4), 285–310.

Muchnik, L., Aral, S., & Taylor, J. (2013). Social influence bias: A randomized experiment. *Science, 341*(6146), 647–651.

Myers, D. G. (1982). Polarizing effect of social interaction. In H. Brandstätter, J. H. Davis, & G. Stocker-Kreichgauger (Eds.), *Group decision making*. Academic Press.

Nowotny, H., Scott, P., & Gibbons, M. (2001). *Re-thinking science: Knowledge and the public in an age of uncertainty*. Cambridge: Policy Press.

Olsson, E. J. (2011, June). A simulation approach to veritistic social epistemology. *Episteme, 8*(2), 127–143.

Polanyi, M. (1958). *Personal knowledge: Towards a post-critical philosophy*. Chicago: University Of Chicago Press.

Pariser, E. (2011). *The filter bubble: What the internet is hiding from you*. New York: Penguin Books.

Rabin, M. (1998). Psychology and Economics. *Journal of Economic Literature, 36*, 11–46.

Rendsvig, R. K., & Hendricks, V. F. (2014). Social proof in extensive games. *The Review of Symbolic Logic*. forthcoming.

Rip, A. (1988). *Contextual changes in contemporary science*. The Netherlands: University of Twente.

Rip, A. (2009, July). Futures of ELSA: Science and society series on convergence research. *EMBO Reports, 10*(7), 666–670.

Robinson, M. (2010). *The privatization of neuroscience: the university, the state and the moral aims of science*. Somatosphere.net. Accessed 11 Jan 2011.

Schelling, T. C. (1960). *The strategy of conflict*. Cambridge: Harvard University Press.

Schelling, T. C. (1978). *Micromotives and macrobehavior*. New York: W. W. Norton Smith.

Schelling, T. C. (1981). Economic reasoning and the ethics of policy. *Public Interest, 63*, 37–61.

Soros, G. (2007). *The age of fallibility*. New York: Public Affairs.

Spalding, J. (2012). *Con art—Why you ought to sell your Damien Hirst's while you can*. CreateSpace Independent Publishing Platform.

Sunstein, C. R. (2002). The law of group polarization. *The Journal of Political Philosophy, 10*(2), 175–195.

Sunstein, C. R. (2006). *Infotopia: How many minds produce knowledge*. Oxford: Oxford University Press.

Sunstein, C. R. (2009). *Going to extremes: How like minds unite and divide*. Oxford: Oxford University Press.

Sunstein, C. R. (2014). Cass Sunstein: 5 Answers. In V. F. Hendricks & R. K. Rendsvig.

Stasavage, D. (2007). Polarization and publicity: Rethinking the benefits of deliberative democracy. *Journal of Politics, 69*(1), 59–72.

Titmuss, R. M. (1971). *The gift relationship: From human blood to social policy*. New Press; Exp Sub edition.

Tversky, A., & Kahneman, D. (1981). The framing of decisions and the psychology of choice. *Science, 211*, 453–458.

Vogel, H. L. (2010). *Financial market bubbles and crashes*. New York: Cambridge University Press.

Weber, A. A. 2009. Weber says ECB has used room to cut interest rates. http://www.bloomberg.com. Accessed May 2013.

Weingart, P. (2005). Impact of bibliometrics upon the science system: Inadvertent consequences?. *Scientometrics, 62*(1), 117–131.

Wadman, M. (2013). Behind the scenes of a brain-mapping moon shot. *Nature Online*. http://www.nature.com. Accessed 6 March 2013.

Ziman, J. M. (2001). Getting scientists to think about what they are doing. *Science and Engineering Ethics, 7*(2), 235–256.

Zuh, H. (2009). Group polarization on corporate boards: Theory and evidence on board decisions about acquisition premiums, executive compensation, and diversification. PhD- Dissertation, The University of Michigan.

Index

V. F. Hendricks, P. G. Hansen, *Infostorms,* DOI 10.1007/978-3-319-03832-2,
© Springer International Publishing Switzerland 2014